UNITED ARE BACK!
LEEDS UNITED 2020/21
BACK IN THE PREMIER LEAGUE
BEHIND CLOSED DOORS

T0315671

First Published in Great Britain in 2020 by DB Publishing, an imprint of JMD Media Ltd

ISBN 9781780916262

Printed and bound in the UK

UNITED ARE BACK!
LEEDS UNITED 2020/21
BACK IN THE PREMIER LEAGUE
BEHIND CLOSED DOORS

HEIDI HAIGH

Heidi's Dedication

This book is dedicated to the memory of another three Leeds United legends, Peter Lorimer, Mick Bates and Terry Cooper, who sadly died during the last year. It is also dedicated to the many Leeds fans who died during the season as well as those of our supporters who are fighting serious health issues. Keep fighting, everyone.

Blog – Follow Me and Leeds United

Welcome back to all my followers for the 2020/21 blog *Follow Me and Leeds United* from me, Heidi Haigh. I am a home and away season ticket holder, a Leeds fan of over 50 years and author of seven Leeds United books. The blog is normally based on my travels to games although this season has been unprecedented with them played behind closed doors. All views are my own and not meant to reflect on anyone else. I am happy for anyone to share these reflections with other fans and always try to respond to comments in good time. LUFC – Marching on Together!

Author of the following books:

Follow Me and Leeds United

Once a Leeds Fan, Always a Leeds Fan

Co-author with Andrew Dalton of *The Good, The Bad and The Ugly of Leeds United: Leeds United in the 1980s*

The Sleeping Giant Awakens 2016/17

Back to Reality: Leeds United 2017/18

Marcelo Bielsa's Leeds United: Leeds United 2018/19

Leeds Are Going to the Premier League! Leeds United Season 2019/20: Promotion in their Centenary Year!

All books are available via my publisher:

https://www.jmdmedia.co.uk/collections/football-clubs/leeds-united-fc

Meet the author: https://www.jmdmedia.co.uk/pages/heidi-haigh-leeds-united

Website: www.followmeandleedsunited.co.uk

Twitter: FollowMeAndLUFC

Facebook: Follow Me and Leeds United

Instagram: Heidi Haigh/Email: lufcheidi@followmeandleedsunited

LinkedIn: Heidi Haigh/Group: Follow Me and Leeds United

Follow Me & Leeds United

ONCE A LEEDS FAN *Always a Leeds fan*

HAIGH

THE GOOD, THE BAD AND THE UGLY
OF LEEDS UNITED
Leeds United in the **1980s**

THE SLEEPING GIANT AWAKENS
LEEDS UNITED 2016-17

BACK TO REALITY!
LEEDS UNITED 2017-18

MARCELO BIELSA'S LEEDS UNITED
LEEDS UNITED 2018-19
HEIDI HAIGH

LEEDS ARE GOING TO THE PREMIER LEAGUE!
LEEDS UNITED SEASON 2019-20
PROMOTION IN THEIR CENTENARY YEAR!
HEIDI HAIGH

HEIDI HAIGH

CONTENTS

Photo courtesy of Phillip Thumbs Up Cresswell

FOREWORD

BY PHILLIP 'THUMBS UP' CRESSWELL

HONOURED

In our first season without four legends too – Norman Hunter, Trevor Cherry, Jack Charlton, and Peter Lorimer. Rest in peace.

What a strange season to have worked at Elland Road after 29 seasons. Hopefully my 30th will be better for everyone. I am gutted for our beloved supporters missing our first season back in the Premier League after 16 years of hurt, and honoured to have been allowed to work the behind-closed-doors games, escorting the away directors after temperature checks in the East Stand reception then to their allocated areas in the West Stand. Along with the majority of staff allowed to work the games, due to COVID-19 protocols, we could only watch the games on TV like our supporters themselves. The season overall was beyond my expectations with Leeds United finishing in a respectable ninth place.

But to be honest, since our football club has gained Mr Radrizzani, Mr Orta, and Mr Kinnear they have put belief and honesty into our wildest expectations. Also the God, Mr Bielsa, who himself has made boys into men on the playing surface. I was extremely impressed by our home results against the so called 'Big Six' and can only imagine a full rocking Elland Road would have put fear into the opposition. I was honoured to be escorting an Arsenal director alongside David O'Leary and his daughter, and he stated that the Premier League has missed Leeds United, the club, and the fans.

Let us hope and pray in August 2021 that Elland Road is rocking again. You Leeds fans deserve it, as football without fans is non-negotiable!

I have missed you all; until we meet again!

Phil Cresswell

Hopefully about to start my 30th season at Elland Road and 27th season at away games.

PROLOGUE

WITH Leeds United promoted from the Championship at the end of the 2019/20 season, it had been gutting not being able to be at the games and celebrate with the team. Never in a million years would I have expected that our first season back in the Premier League, would see games played behind closed doors rather than have fans in attendance due to the COVID-19 pandemic. Not being at all the home and away games has hit hard as normally when times are tough, being with our football family is what gets me through. As it is, luckily, we have been able to watch all the games televised live so have seen what a great season Leeds United have had. Once again, we have played some fantastic football under Marcelo Bielsa, and finished the season well.

At the start of the season, I was on BBC Radio 5 Live alongside a Fulham and West Bromwich Albion fan who also saw their teams promoted. I was asked where I expected Leeds to finish in the table, but I would not give a prediction. My comments were that we aim for the top as in Premier League winners. Not that I expected Leeds to win the league but aiming for the top of the table meant that if you did not win it, you had the chance to play in Europe with the places below. Failing that, you ended up in mid-table. I was still pushed to give a specific place and I said we should not aim for 17th place as there are only relegation places below you. Interestingly, Leeds finished in a respectable ninth place, so aiming for the top was correct. The other two fans predicted their teams should aim for 17th place and were both relegated – so I rest my case!

Leeds had a lot of injuries throughout the early part of the season which impacted on a settled side. There was a definite difference in how we played once key players were back in the team but once again, they never gave up. They played with pride wearing the Leeds United shirt and there is a fantastic team spirit where they play and fight for each other. That is something that was missing for such a long time, and it is great to see the passion of the fans replicated throughout the team.

This book takes you on the journey of our games through the eyes of me, Heidi Haigh, despite not being there in person due to circumstances beyond my control. There were plenty of highs and lows as the season progressed, but I had every faith that the team would always perform well. The last home game of the season against West Bromwich Albion saw Leeds fans back in the stadium although with a reduced capacity crowd. An emotional send-off for both Gaetano Berardi and Pablo Hernández ensued with this being their last ever game for the club before moving on. I am grateful for being there to capture the photos that are included in this book. Enjoy the read.

FANS' COMMENTS

Mick Glasby, 23 January 2021: review of my book *Leeds Are Going to the Premier League!*

Hi Heidi, I have just finished reading your latest book *Leeds Are Going to the Premier League!* and I have to say that I was blown away in a nice way in what I read. I loved the foreword of Matt and Jack Brown who are definitely in the bracket of top gold Leeds supporters because of the distances they have to cover to follow the Mighty Whites. Two really loving Leeds human beings. I also love the pictures of all our smiling fans and thank you for including me in them. I really took my time reading this book as I wanted to savour every match report of the games and again, although I was at some of them myself where I have to pick certain matches I can afford to go to, being a pensioner and having to watch the pennies. I save up first so that I can then go to a particular match. But with each match report it was like I was at every particular game especially at Elland Road except of course ground closures because of the virus. I know what the atmosphere is like and the positive electricity that is generated by the fans, especially since Marcelo Bielsa has become the club's manager. I know you and I are biased about our much-loved club, but you are bang on about most referees at our games who definitely give many of the opposition players a very unfair advantage in their poor decision-making whether deliberate or not.

But what a great time to get back into the Premier League in our centenary year, just fabulous. An absolutely excellent book. I will go as far as saying your best one I've read of your books. As good as they all are that I've read, it is because of what a great season it was. Always Leeds and Proud MOT.

Ken Lee

Welcome back Heidi, have missed you and your reports.

Jeff Way

Thanks Heidi, really appreciate the time that you take to write these blogs. I am glad you got to see the match live. It was sad to see Pablo and Gaetano leaving the pitch for the last time. I admit I had a tear but having said that what a brilliant season we have had; so proud of each and every one of them with a couple of additions who knows what we can achieve next season have a good summer and look forward to reading some more next season. MOT ALAW.

Sniffer Clarke

Thank you very much for your blog match reports throughout the season, Heidi. I for one very much enjoy reading them and I am sure that is the case for many others here on this page. I hope you enjoyed your day at the game yesterday. It was good to see some fans back in the stadium and what a noise they made. Was also great to finish what has been a fabulous season with a win. MOT.

Mick Glasby

Hi Heidi, yes it was a very emotional last game of the season for both fans and all the players but especially for our Pablo Hernández and Gaetano Berardi. I was thinking of you and all the fans that were lucky enough to be able to get a ticket to watch the game inside our church. I had one of the next best seats watching it in the beer garden at the White Hart, Beeston who had put a marquee up and a big TV screen to watch the match and of course there were lots of Leeds fans there singing and cheering including me who now has a bit of a hoarse voice lol. We the Nottingham Whites who came up had an absolute brilliant time considering we were not actually able to watch the game live inside our church. After the game we walked to the ground and stood outside singing more and more and with some Leeds fans that I met and chatted to who had flown over especially from Dublin. You just cannot beat being in Leeds with other Mighty Whites fans on matchdays. Another great report of the game Heidi where Leeds won the match easily and a great finale to the season. I just hope that Kalvin has not injured himself too badly, he is a great lad and deserves to be in the England squad for the Euros. Hope that he can play. Always Leeds and Proud MOT.

CHAPTER 1 – SEPTEMBER 2020

LIVERPOOL V LEEDS UNITED; 12 SEPTEMBER 2020
AT ANFIELD

With the season finishing only seven weeks ago for Leeds United, the new season started in earnest today with our first game back in the Premier League after a 16-year absence. Sadly, once again this was to be behind closed doors due to the COVID-19 pandemic that still affects our lives. As a fan, not being there was gutting, and I cannot wait for us to get back to going to games with our fantastic fans as I have missed you!

It has been a busy week for me on the media front again, first when I was asked to interview Leif Davis, one of our youngsters, at the Dakota Hotel in Leeds, then appear on *BBC Look North* on Friday. The latter was outside Billy's statue and involved Phil Beeton of the Leeds United Supporters' Club, young fan Josh, Adam Pope, Noel Whelan and I giving a pre-game preview. The next day I appeared on Radio 5 Live at 8.15am alongside a West Bromwich Albion and Fulham fan. Fulham had already been beaten yesterday and WBA were due to play on Sunday. Interestingly, I was the only one aiming for the top and when challenged to give a position, my stance was the following. Aim for the top, then you have the Champions League places below and then other places after that. Aim for just above the relegation places and all you have is relegation.

Team: Meslier, Struijk, Koch (making his debut from Freiburg), Ayling, Dallas, Costa, Hernández, Harrison, Phillips, Klich, Bamford.
Subs: Roberts for Hernández (62), Rodrigo (making his debut from Valencia) for Bamford (62), Shackleton for Klich (81).
Subs not used: Casilla, Poveda, Casey.
Leeds lost the game 4-3 (Liverpool were awarded two penalties, one in the third minute and one in the 88th minute). Harrison (12), Bamford (30) and Klich (66) were the Leeds scorers.
Attendance: Zero, behind closed doors.
Referee: Michael Oliver.

With Liam Cooper having pulled out with an injury received in the internationals that took place this week, that was a blow for him not being able to lead the team out at Anfield on our first game back. I feel having the internationals for the two weeks prior to the start of the new season was very badly timed, although admittedly, it was due to the pandemic. With the injury to Cooper, it meant that our new signing Koch made his debut alongside

Struijk. With Koch himself only returning from international duty with Germany, there was not much time to familiarise himself with the way we play the game.

The game set off at a cracking pace which was understandable, but Leeds were dealt an early blow when the referee blew for a penalty after the ball hit Koch on the hand. After VAR made a quick decision to confirm this, afterwards it was said that according to the new rules it should not have been awarded as the ball deflected off his foot. A very harsh decision to put Leeds on the back foot.

The IFAB rules state: It is not an offence if the ball touches a player's hand/arm directly from the player's own head or body (including the foot)

I felt by Liverpool scoring the early goal, this would at least take the pressure off Leeds, and they could go out and play football. As it was, we took the game to Liverpool. There was a lot of end-to-end football, and it was a great advert for the game, and it showed what Bielsa has brought to Leeds United. Costa got the ball into the net only to see the goal ruled out for offside. That only spurred Leeds on as they attacked once more towards the Kop end with Phillips sending a great ball on to the wing for Harrison. He made it look so easy as he cut inside two men and unleashed a shot that hit the back of the net to equalise with a great goal and our first in the Premier League this season.

Liverpool regained the lead from a corner when it looked like Koch had lost his man, but replays showed he had been blocked and the goal should not have stood. Liverpool were penalised later for the same foul. Once again, though, Leeds came back and after a Bamford chance crept away from him when he tried to go around the keeper, I said to learn from that, and he should have hit it first time. A short while later the same opportunity arose after a poor clearance and this time Bamford made no mistake for Leeds to equalise for the second time on the day. Meslier made a fantastic save after the ball rebounded off Struijk before once again, Liverpool regained the lead for us to go in 3-2 down at half-time.

At the start of the second half, we sat back as Liverpool put us under a lot of pressure before Leeds had a further goal disallowed for offside. After Klich pointed for Costa to place the ball where he wanted it, he sent a great shot into the net for Leeds to equalise for a third time. With the action being fast and furious, you hardly had time to draw breath as the end of the game drew near. When a Liverpool goal was chalked off for being offside, I hoped we could see the game out for a draw. Sadly, they were given a second penalty to win the game after a foul by Rodrigo in the box. Leeds deserved something out of the game as they had played really well in an entertaining game. Although we had not got the deserved point, the team had shown the Premier League what they have been missing with some fantastic football on show. It had the desired effect to have everyone talking about us which grated on many opposition fans' nerves though. Oh dear, what a shame!

It was a baptism of fire today but with Cooper out through injury, we had two centre-backs who had not played together apart from the last three days. In reality, Liverpool needed two penalties to win on the day so be proud of the way we played and next time, they won't be so lucky!

LUFC – Marching on Together!

LEEDS UNITED V HULL CITY; CARABAO CUP SECOND ROUND, 16 SEPTEMBER 2020
AT ELLAND ROAD

Leeds made many changes to the team today and although I know it gives the fringe and young players a chance of a game, I felt there were more changes than normal. It is a shame that we do not try to progress in this cup competition especially when there is a chance to compete in Europe again. With this being the first game back at Elland Road that we were not allowed to attend, this also hit hard, and I hated having to watch it on TV which was soul destroying. With there being no sound behind the commentary too, it was horrible to watch. From a Leeds fan's perspective, that also included the way we were playing.

Team: Casilla, Cresswell, Douglas, Davis, Casey, Bogusz, Roberts, Poveda, Alioski, Rodrigo, Shackleton.
Subs: Struijk for Casey (45), Gotts for Bogusz (78).
Subs not used: Meslier, Bamford, Harrison, Phillips, McCalmont.
The score after 90 minutes was 1-1 with Alioski equalising on 90+3. Leeds lost the game 9-8 on penalties.
Attendance: Zero, behind closed doors.
Referee: David Webb.
Booked: Alioski.

With ex-Leeds players Mallik Wilks and Lewie Coyle (captain for the game) in the Hull side, it was no surprise to see Wilks score within five minutes with a deflected shot. I am sure he felt he had a point to prove. Hull were doing all the early attacking, putting Leeds under pressure and after our first corner, they counter-attacked with Wilks once again, with a deflected shot, coming close to scoring a second. The nearest Leeds came to scoring was in the closing minutes of the half when Alioski's shot went over the bar.

The second half saw Struijk come on to replace Casey, but it was at least 20 minutes before Hull had a couple more chances to score with Casilla being called into action to save one. With Hull having most of the game they should have put it to bed with four minutes to go. Their player had only Casilla to beat but he rose to the challenge and stopped him. With that Leeds had a shot from Gotts saved which was our first shot on target during the game. With injury time ticking away I just knew Leeds were going to score to take the game to penalties and it was Alioski who smashed the ball home to equalise.

Leeds were taking penalties first with Rodrigo getting his first goal for Leeds with the first one. Alioski's penalty bounced back off the post so missed, but Roberts, Poveda and

Douglas scored, and it was 4-4 before sudden death due to Coyle missing his penalty. Struijk, Davis, Gotts and Casilla were successful with their penalties but when Shackleton missed, Hull scored the deciding penalty to take them through on the night. With a bad game from our point of view at least it livened up at the end.

With Mark Jackson set to take over as coach of the under-23s, hopefully the way of everyone playing the same way will take on a new lease of life. Back to league action on Saturday with our first home Premier League game, it will be a different game altogether.

LUFC – Marching on Together!

LEEDS UNITED V FULHAM; 19 SEPTEMBER 2020 AT ELLAND ROAD

Having been contacted prior to the game by someone from Cable+, the equivalent to SKY TV in France, I signposted them to the Whistlestop and Millennium Square in Leeds. They were wanting to meet some of the fans and hear them out after what was hoped to be our first win this season. Hopefully, they met plenty!

Team: Meslier, Cooper (back from injury and captaining Leeds for his first game in the Premier League), Dallas, Koch, Rodrigo (making his Premier League start due to Hernández being injured in the pre-game warm up), Bamford, Costa, Harrison, Klich, Phillips, Ayling. Subs: Roberts for Rodrigo (45), Alioski for Bamford (70).

Subs not used: Caprile, Struijk, Bogusz, Shackleton, Poveda.

Leeds won the game 4-3 with goals from Costa (5 and 57), Klich (penalty 41) and Bamford (50). Attendance: Zero, behind closed doors.

Referee: Kevin Friend.

Booked: Klich.

Leeds took an early lead when we scored from a corner. Phillips sent the ball into the middle, which was headed on to Costa all on his own at the back post where he smashed the ball into the net via the underside of the crossbar. After a chance from Fulham, Leeds came close again when the keeper made a save from Koch after another corner. Leeds were dealt a blow when another penalty was awarded against us after a challenge from Koch. To me he had already pulled out of the challenge and was unlucky to slightly connect with their player. Fulham scored from it to equalise with Meslier unlucky not to save it when he went the right way. That was not the end of the drama in the first half though as Bamford was pushed in the back to prevent a scoring chance and Leeds were awarded a penalty. Klich duly put the penalty away and Leeds went into the break leading 2-1 after Meslier kept Fulham out with a save.

In the second half Leeds went further ahead after a great pass from Klich to Bamford saw him put the ball into the net in front of the Kop. After another attack Bamford, on the left wing towards the Kop, sent a great pass across the penalty area and Costa hit an unstoppable shot into the net. It was great to see Leeds scoring goals as the Fulham defence just seemed to stop and watch Costa again in space get the ball.

At times we had not been strong enough in midfield for me, with Roberts being bundled off the ball giving Fulham some hope. Suddenly they were able to get back into the game when they got past Phillips and with their player already past Dallas, they went on to score. They got a further goal from a cross into the middle as Meslier looked to be blinded by the sun and went back on to his line, as their player rose above Cooper to head into the goal. The comfortable end to the game that was anticipated was suddenly under pressure especially when Fulham hit another shot that I think was covered by Meslier but hit the post and went wide. Bielsa then changed things by bringing Alioski on and he was unlucky not to score but was denied by the keeper who also kept out the rebound from Roberts. With Meslier saving a shot from Fulham, we were able to see the game out to get our first win and three points of the season.

Another entertaining game with plenty of goals, and despite many having worries about conceding seven goals already, we must remember three of those were penalties. We will be fine as we continue to play together and will go from strength to strength. Once again, the plaudits are for the way we are playing and Bielsa will continue to play the way we do. Our best form of defence is attack Leeds which shows when we keep the ball away from the opposition. Minimising playing across the back which I know needs to be done at times and for instance, when all we needed to do was turn and take the attack back up the field, we see the ball hit a long way back to Meslier, we will not go far wrong. Please get us back to games soon.

LUFC – Marching on Together!

SHEFFIELD UNITED V LEEDS UNITED; 27 SEPTEMBER 2020 AT BRAMALL LANE

On 25 September we heard the sad news that another player from my early days of following Leeds, Peter Hampton, had died whilst on holiday in Cyprus with his family after his recent retirement. I remember him as one of the Leeds United youngsters but then it was a shock to realise he was only slightly older than I am now. My thoughts are with his family at this time.

Leeds have still been busy in the transfer market having signed another defender Diego Llorente from Real Sociedad, who is a Spanish international player and will play with number 14 on his back.

Team: Meslier, Koch, Phillips, Ayling, Dallas, Cooper, Costa, Roberts, Bamford, Klich, Harrison.
Subs: Rodrigo for Roberts (45), Poveda for Costa (65), Alioski for Rodrigo (90+1).
Subs not used: Caprile, Shackleton, Davis, Struijk.
Leeds won the game 1-0 with a goal by Bamford (88).
Attendance: Zero, behind closed doors.
Referee: Paul Tierney.
Booked: Phillips.

I had no preconceptions about how the game would go but once again I was adamant that Leeds should go out and play the best they can and still aim for the top, never giving up. Leeds nearly got off to a great start when Ayling's great shot was saved by their keeper to prevent an early goal. Sheffield had a shot that went wide before a Bamford header at the other end went over the bar. I said that Bamford should not worry as he will do better next time. He did come closer with his next header so I said that it would be third time lucky for him. Meslier then made a fantastic save to prevent Sheffield going in front when the ball looked destined to be a goal. Dallas was the next to come close when their keeper made another save to prevent us taking the lead. The teams went into the break on even terms thanks to another save from Meslier. The whistle blew and for once I had not even looked at the clock to see how long was left. Although it was quite tight between the two teams, the first half had passed quickly.

Rodrigo came on in place of Roberts for the second half and Leeds started off on the attack where Costa and Bamford both had shots saved. Meslier was called into action again and showing how competent he was with another save. He is coming on in leaps and bounds and I feel very comfortable with him in goal. When Dallas rounded the keeper after a great pass from Ayling, sadly there was not enough power on the ball and their player cleared it off the line. Dallas produced a great pass that saw a header from Rodrigo go over the bar. I thought then that he would work well with Bamford who will learn how to direct his headers better. After some great work from Poveda, again their keeper made the save.

Once Sheffield brought two subs on in McBurnie and Sharp with 16 minutes to go, Leeds began to have more room when attacking. As long as we kept them out, I knew we would keep fighting until the end so stood a chance of winning the game. A draw would not be a disgrace but obviously three points are better than one. Sheffield saw a chance go wide before Meslier dived at the feet of their player only to receive a bad challenge in his stomach despite their player trying to pull out of the challenge. With another attack after a great run from Harrison, his cross was met in the middle by Bamford to head the ball into the net to put Leeds into the lead with two minutes of normal time remaining. That had me dancing about the room shouting get in, to Bamford and third time lucky with the header! Alioski was brought on for Rodrigo as Leeds saw out five minutes of injury time to take the win and three points.

Well done lads, that is just the tonic we needed. I cannot wait to get back to the grounds in person to support you on the terraces as it cannot come soon enough for me and I'm sure the same feelings are with thousands more Leeds United fans. With two home games coming next against Man City and Wolves, I am looking forward to Leeds getting stronger with more game time.

LUFC – Marching on Together!

CHAPTER 2 – OCTOBER 2020

LEEDS UNITED V MANCHESTER CITY; 3 OCTOBER 2020 AT ELLAND ROAD

Today was always going to be a tough game with Bielsa coming up against his disciple Pep Guardiola. Having had a hectic week and as usual only concentrating on Leeds United, I kept seeing before the game today that we were going to get hammered. As usual, I said we need to play to our strengths, keep fighting and never giving up and we could finish the game strongly with a win. Whatever happens we would not be hammered in my opinion.

Team: Meslier, Cooper, Dallas, Koch, Phillips, Bamford, Costa, Roberts, Klich, Alioski, Bamford.
Subs: Poveda for Alioski (45), Rodrigo for Roberts (56), Davis for Klich (77).
Subs not used: Caprile, Llorente, Struijk, Shackleton.
Leeds drew the game 1-1 with Rodrigo equalising for Leeds (59) after City had taken a 17th-minute lead through Sterling. Attendance: Zero, behind closed doors.
Referee: Mike Dean.
Booked: Dallas, Bamford.

With heavy rain before the game from Storm Alex, it showed no signs of abating, so the pitch was very heavy although it looked in great shape. The first 20 minutes saw Leeds under the cosh from City and it looked like they had scored from a free kick with Meslier beaten, only for our luck to hold with the ball hitting the post and back into play before going wide for a corner. Leeds were unable to get much play going, had to defend most of the time and it felt like we were in awe of them. They had quite a few chances before we had an attack and Alioski got into a great position, but his header went over the top.

With Dallas stopping a shot on the line to keep us level, we succumbed a few minutes later when City took the lead. When I said to my other half that we would be able to play now as that had taken the pressure off us again as per Liverpool, he pulled a face at me. I said to him that it would, and I was proved right. Although City still had a lot of the game, Leeds started to make inroads with attacks on their goal firstly]'[, Bamford had a shot that went wide and then with Dallas through their keeper made the save to keep him out. After another City chance, Leeds nearly got an equaliser just before the break when Ayling pounced on a defensive mistake but was denied by a great stop by their keeper. The signs were there that Leeds were starting to get into the game as we went into the break a goal down.

Bielsa started to change things at the start of the second half by bringing on Poveda to replace Alioski. Straight away Poveda ran down the wing putting City under pressure and lifting the Leeds players (and supporters no doubt). I like his attitude a great deal and he has a lot of skill for a recent newcomer to our team. When Rodrigo came on to replace Roberts, he added a bit more steel into the team and within two minutes came close to equalising as Leeds counter-attacked, with his deflected shot going over the crossbar resulting in a corner. When the corner came into the middle of the goal area, the keeper did not clear the ball which landed at Rodrigo's feet for him to hit the ball into the net to equalise. My screams of joy did not go down well with my hubby's hearing, so I had to tone it down a bit. Oops.

With Phillips having a shot saved and Cooper's header hitting the post, it was Rodrigo's turn to come close when their keeper made a fantastic save to tip the ball on to the post to stop us taking the lead. City started to get back into the game after a substitution and with only Meslier to beat it looked like they were going to take the lead again. Meslier stood firm and eventually was able to grab the ball from his feet to prevent it. As the minutes counted down to the final whistle, I decided I was not going to cross my fingers until the end of the game. I was going to be positive as I kicked every ball with the team, willed them on with every attack and fought for every ball. It was end-to-end for a lot of the game as first City had a chance to win the game and then Bamford with a last chance for us, saw it saved once again by their keeper as the final whistle blew.

That was a great result for us today and as always, I am proud of the Leeds United team and proud to be a Leeds United supporter. Although we could have snatched a win at the death, a draw was a good result and today also shows that we can play against the best with players costing millions more than ours. One thing I have noticed from playing in the Premier League is the standard of refereeing. Although I still do not agree with every decision they make, there has been a better flow of the game rather than stop-start for every challenge made. Admittedly they have not refereed a game in front of a crowd as yet, but hopefully that will still be maintained when they do.

I am sure there are many more fans like myself who cannot wait to get back to the games and will be up for attending in person sooner rather than later. If you want volunteers, Leeds, then please do not hesitate to ask me! Hope to see you all soon.

LUFC – Marching on Together!

LEEDS UNITED V WOLVERHAMPTON WANDERERS; 19 OCTOBER 2020 AT ELLAND ROAD

Another game that fans cannot attend after the planned reduced crowds ended up on the back burner. Sadly, there seems to be no sign of a light at the end of that tunnel at this moment. My thoughts go out to the friends and families of some of our Leeds United

supporters who have died recently. Being together to help others through hard times is sorely missed.

After the recent international games saw some of our players return early, it looks like precautionary measures were in place. At this moment in time, I would happily give up the international games and let us concentrate on league games instead although I am sure there are many fans who would disagree with me!

Leeds have just celebrated their 101st birthday this week. Having seen a video appear on my timeline of me taking a penalty against Lucas the Kop Cat, at last year's Birmingham centenary game, I could not help but laugh. It was a case of mind your heads as the ball whizzed past some heads into the East Stand, oh dear.

Team: Meslier, Struijk, Koch, Ayling, Dallas, Costa, Harrison, Klich, Phillips, Rodrigo, Bamford.
Subs: Poveda for Costa (71), Hernández for Struijk (75), Raphinha for Harrison (82).
Subs not used: Casilla, Alioski, Shackleton, Roberts.
Attendance: Zero, behind closed doors.
Leeds lost the game 1-0.
Referee: David Coote.
Booked: Ayling, Phillips.

After hearing that Cooper had to pull out of the game after a recurrence of the groin injury which possibly was aggravated in the international game too, Struijk ended up starting. Leeds had plenty of possession in the first half and were playing some good attacking football. With one of their players on the floor after Phillips's hand caught him in the face, to me it looked tame. I was shouting at their player to get up and stop making a meal of it. I then saw the blood on his finger and thought okay, maybe he has got a reason to stay down after all. After a good move, Bamford headed the ball into the net, but I knew it wasn't going to be allowed for offside. Go on Patrick, we will have a hat-trick from you instead was my cry. Just before half-time Wolves looked as if they were going to score but Meslier made a vital save as we went into the break on equal terms.

After having most of the possession in the first half, Wolves came out of the starting blocks with a point to prove. Leeds were being put under pressure and Wolves scored what looked to be a good goal from the edge of the area. As I was saying damn, VAR made the decision that they had been offside in the build-up to the goal and it was disallowed luckily for us. Ayling and Phillips were booked. I thought that we should be looking to change our game but then thought that Bielsa will do that when he is ready. Hopefully, it is a case of letting Wolves have their ten minutes and we will get back on top.

By the time we did make a change we were a goal down due to an own goal by Phillips. This was due to Wolves getting a couple of slices of luck with first Struijk slipping but he managed to get back in position, then their player keeping hold of the ball which ended up

with them scoring. Costa made way for Poveda and then Hernández came on for Struijk who was injured earlier. It meant we had to reshuffle at the back as Leeds tried to get back into the game. Raphinha came on for Harrison and Leeds had been unlucky not to score just before that when Hernández's shot was deflected over the bar. Another good chance slipped us by, but the final ball bounced over our player. After Koch fouled their player, the latter was lucky not to get a red card after kicking out and catching Koch as he tried to get out of the way. The longer the game went on, I just knew that we were not going to equalise. We deserved at least a point but need to move on to Friday's game and make amends.

LUFC – Marching on Together!

ASTON VILLA V LEEDS UNITED; 23 OCTOBER 2020 AT VILLA PARK

I had originally put this down as a home game in my diary by mistake and even though I had changed it, I was still convinced we were playing at home. I would not have thought that if I'd been going to the game though! When I heard that Villa had a 100 per cent record so far this season, I really hoped we could be the ones to beat them.

Team: Meslier, Ayling, Alioski, Struijk, Bamford, Rodrigo, Dallas, Costa, Harrison, Klich, Koch.

Subs: Shackleton for Struijk (21), Hernández for Rodrigo (79), Raphinha for Costa (83).

Subs not used: Casilla, Roberts, Davis, Poveda.

Leeds won the game 3-0 with a hat-trick from Bamford (55, 67 and 74).

Attendance: Zero, behind closed doors.

Referee: Paul Tierney.

Booked: Struijk, Klich.

Leeds started the game well with first Bamford's header going narrowly wide and Alioski's shot saved by the Villa keeper. Villa had a chance before Struijk ended up with an early booking after a foul on Grealish. After he made a second tackle on Grealish which saw normal service resume from Grealish in diving and cheating, trying to get Struijk sent off, Bielsa made a tactical decision to bring Shackleton on. Nurturing the young lad was a good move and to ensure we kept 11 men on the pitch too. Grealish could actually be a good footballer if he took a leaf out of our players' books, by staying on his feet and cutting out the cheating. Because of this, I cannot stand him as a player, give me our honest players any day.

The change made a difference to the way we had been playing and put us more on the back foot for a while. It looked like Villa were going to take the lead when Grealish beat Meslier, but Ayling made a goal-line clearance to keep us in the game. Bamford had a shot

blocked and Rodrigo's shot went over the crossbar before VAR was brought in to check whether Villa should have a penalty, but this went in our favour. Leeds' best chance of the game came just before half-time after a great run from Harrison saw him cross the ball into the middle, but Bamford's shot went wide. It was nice to see us finish the half strongly.

Leeds started the second half well too with Harrison on another great run down the left, bringing a save out of their keeper. Leeds were lucky not to be punished when Grealish went on a run and Meslier made a great save to prevent Villa taking the lead. As Villa piled on the pressure, I started to get the jitters and thought we may have to change things when Meslier made another save to keep them out. Bielsa decided otherwise and he was right because another run from Harrison down the wing saw him cross the ball to Rodrigo. His shot was parried by the keeper and Bamford got to the rebound first and slammed the ball into the net to put us into the lead. After a challenge with Mings, Bamford went down in the penalty area hurt. Although VAR concluded it was no penalty, Mings should have had a second yellow for man-handling Bamford, grabbing his shirt, and dragging him off the floor. Oh dear, Mings, what a shame, you got Bamford that mad that he scored two more cracking goals to get a hat-trick! His second was a cracking shot from the edge of the box after a great pass from Klich. Klich himself had a shot saved by the keeper before Bamford completed his hat-trick with a third sublime goal. Rodrigo sent the ball out to Costa on the wing, who passed to Shackleton in the penalty area. His ball came to Bamford with four defenders around him and he switched feet and sent a fantastic shot into the top left of the goal to give us a great score line away from home! That was it, game over although Villa did have one shot that whistled over the crossbar, but Meslier had it covered. Hernández had a great chance to get a fourth in the closing stages of the game only to put the ball over the top of the goal.

That was a great win for Leeds, and I also feel that Bamford and Rodrigo will have a great partnership. With Bamford not on his own at the front, that will put more pressure on the opposition. The three points sees Leeds beat Villa on their doorstep to stop their record start to the season and their unbeaten run. Although the rest of the teams have still to play this weekend, it was still nice seeing us in third place in the Premier League with ten points. As I have said before, aim for the top Leeds and you never know what happens!

LUFC – Marching on Together!

CHAPTER 3 – NOVEMBER 2020

LEEDS UNITED V LEICESTER CITY; 2 NOVEMBER 2020
AT ELLAND ROAD

With another lockdown looming this week, getting back to football games seems a long way away. Having gone past the ground today, knowing it was a match day and I could not go to the game tonight hit hard. I am missing Elland Road and my friends so much.

A minute's silence was held for Nobby Stiles, who was the brother-in-law of Johnny Giles, and his son John Stiles played for Leeds. He was part of the squad alongside Jack Charlton who won the World Cup with England in 1966. He was also another player who had dementia, which made me think of those hard medicine balls that footballers in that era used to play with. As today was also the nearest home game to Armistice Day, 'The Last Post' was played in remembrance of all those who died whilst serving their country and to pay our respects. It was poignant seeing the remembrance flag in the East Stand too.

Team: Meslier, Cooper, Ayling, Koch, Hernández, Costa, Klich, Harrison, Bamford, Dallas, Shackleton.
Subs: Poveda for Shackleton (45), Roberts for Hernández (67), Alioski for Dallas (81).
Subs not used: Casilla, Struijk, Casey, Davis.
Leeds lost the game 4-1 with Dallas scoring the Leeds goal (48). Attendance: Zero, behind closed doors.
Referee: Andre Marriner.
Booked: Dallas.

With Rodrigo pulling out due to COVID reasons, it meant Leeds had to reshuffle the team, although Cooper was back after injury. Leeds came close after Costa crossed for Harrison at the far post, who headed back to Bamford in the middle only for his header to go straight to the keeper. Leicester immediately counter-attacked as their keeper threw the ball out. With Leeds under pressure, Koch sent a back pass which went straight to Vardy who passed back to his player to put the ball into the net, to see Leeds a goal down after two minutes. That was a bad goal to concede especially so early on, giving us an uphill battle.

Leeds came very close to conceding a second goal shortly after. Meslier then made a great save to keep out another chance after Dallas looked to be fouled on the far touchline, but the referee played on. Dallas was limping for a short while afterwards. Leeds put pressure on Leicester with a great run by Costa on the right, who passed the ball into the middle

but Bamford's shot under pressure went wide. With heavy conditions due to the rain, Leeds were guilty of some bad passing and were putting pressure on ourselves.

Bielsa changed the formation to put an extra man in defence but Leicester were dictating the play. Meslier made another great save from Vardy with Koch beaten but the rebound was put into the net to give Leicester a second goal. This feels like a game which was crying out for the Leeds fans to be a 12th man. As our players kept slipping on the heavy pitch, maybe we needed a change of football boots at half-time! When one of the Leicester players was sandwiched between Costa and another, I was expecting the free kick to be given but the referee played on. When Leeds got on what looked to be a good attack with Shackleton through, the whistle blew for offside, as the rebound came to Costa. It is not the end of the world Leeds, keep fighting was my cry. At this moment though, we do look like the newcomers to the division as Leicester are looking a very accomplished side.

Klich cleared the ball as far as Costa who then lost the ball and Meslier saved the shot from Leicester. Leeds came so close to getting a goal back when Ayling's pass to Bamford beat the defence, but he could not get a first shot in and the keeper smothered the ball. Harrison's cross saw their player put the ball out for a corner, but we wasted it. We had started to get into more attacking positions just before half-time but without getting a shot on goal. Leicester broke away but Leeds won the ball back luckily to prevent another attack. We won another corner which Leicester cleared with ease from Hernández. Leeds won a free kick when Costa was brought down near the byline just before the break, but we went in two goals down.

Poveda came on for Shackleton at the start of the half as Leeds looked to get back into the game. We won an early corner but this time it was Klich and Harrison who took a short corner. I am not normally a lover of short corners, but we had to do something different, and Dallas's shot went over everyone straight into the net to pull a goal back at the Kop end. Leeds came so close to getting a second one after another short corner, only for Hernández's shot to come back off the top-right corner of the goal. Leeds had a long-range shot on target from Klich that was saved by their keeper. Leicester then made a sub to change things as Leeds had been on top for most of the second half. Not long after, Roberts came on for Hernández and the latter was very disappointed to be subbed. Bamford was through on goal but with their keeper bearing down on him near the edge of the penalty area, he pulled out of the challenge. When Ayling looked to be brought down in the area I thought it was a penalty straight away, but the referee said no. Replays showed he had made the right decision. A breakaway goal then by Vardy for Leicester after Roberts lost possession meant we had an even more uphill battle now with the score at 3-1. Alioski came on for Dallas as Bielsa tried changing things again. Leeds won another corner but the corner from Harrison was cleared easily by the defence. With Vardy through again, we had Meslier to thank for making the save to keep him out. Poveda was brought down just as Vardy was taken off and another defender brought on

as Leicester looked to keep the lead. VAR made the decision three minutes after a challenge to bring the game back to be looked at again. After the referee checked, he decided it was a penalty after all as their player was brought down on the edge of the box by Klich. As the ball was not even in the area, how could that be a penalty? There again, I thought to myself, with not being to a live game since March, had I forgotten the rules for a penalty in that their player was on the line? Personally, I know I am biased, but I could not agree with the penalty decision, but we were now 4-1 down and it was game over. Despite losing by the margin, we did, it could have been a different game if Hernández's shot had gone into the net. We will have our ups and downs this season, just like last, but we just need to keep fighting and never give up, getting as many points as we can along the way.

Take care everyone and if you feel that things are getting so bad for you, please reach out to the other Leeds fans in our lives to help you through it.

LUFC – Marching on Together.

CRYSTAL PALACE V LEEDS UNITED; 7 NOVEMBER 2020 AT SELHURST PARK

Good news, my new book is out – *Leeds Are Going to the Premier League! Leeds United Season 2019-20: Promotion in their Centenary Year!* Just in time for Christmas presents or as a distraction to read through lockdown. Books can be bought direct from my publisher at www.jmdmedia.co.uk using HAIGH25 code to get a discount.

Sadly, not being able to go to games in person now where I normally meet fans to sign books for them makes things harder. Please note that once we are allowed back, I am happy to meet up with fans and sign books that are bought from any outlet. Whilst I am still waiting to receive my own stock of books, I am happy to sign them, but postage and packing will be added to any costs. I also do have a small amount of my previous books if anyone is interested in purchasing them as well.

With a London game on the horizon, I would not miss the early morning get-up and long journey, but I do miss being amongst our fans travelling to the game and watching the team. As someone pointed out this morning that Leeds get a nosebleed going further than Watford Gap, I said we had to forget where we were and think we were playing in Yorkshire. Damn, it still didn't work having a positive, mental attitude.

Going to Selhurst Park brought back some memories for me, firstly going there when we played Wimbledon in an FA Cup replay. We could not get over the pink tiles in the ladies' toilets and the mirrors on the walls. For those fans who used to go to games in the 1970s, they will know these were the height of luxury in those days. The other game was playing Charlton in the play-offs. We were stuck on the M1 for two hours after a car crashed into the back of a coach, killing some Leeds fans sadly. It stopped all the traffic. We did not get there until half-time and I had such a migraine by the time we arrived that I could not enjoy the game. I think it is a horrible ground to get to when travelling from the north.

Team: Meslier, Ayling Cooper, Koch, Alioski, Struijk, Costa, Klich, Dallas, Harrison, Bamford.

Subs: Raphinha for Costa (45), Roberts for Struijk (71).

Subs not used: Casilla, Davis, Casey, Jenkins, Poveda.

Leeds lost the game 4-1 with Bamford scoring our goal (27).

Attendance: Zero, behind closed doors.

Referee: Chris Kavanagh.

Booked: Cooper, Klich.

With Hernández not even on the bench, people were thinking it was down to his dissent last week when he was subbed. Palace were straight on the attack and Meslier saved a good shot in the opening minutes. As Leeds battled to get the ball away near the touchline, the ball hit their player's hand, but no free kick was given. Palace got into another great position to shoot not long after, but Alioski nicked the ball off their player's toes to clear. Meslier was called into action again to make the save. Leeds got a corner in the seventh minute which

was taken by Klich, but Cooper's header went over the top of the goal. Cooper went in hard to win the ball and as I held my breath expecting a free kick, the referee played on. I feel that the game is more free flowing in the Premier League with more common sense applied which is good to see after the appalling standard of refereeing we have had to put up with in the Championship. That said, it now looks like VAR has taken over from that!

Palace took the lead from a corner with an unstoppable header that deflected slightly off Koch's head into the top right-hand corner of the goal despite Meslier trying his hardest to keep it out. Leeds then went on the attack but did not put their keeper under pressure. We tried again and Harrison should have hit the ball first time, but Palace won the ball back, so we lost the opportunity. We equalised with a goal from Bamford after a great pass from Klich which saw him beat the defence to lift the ball over the keeper. I could not believe what happened next, as VAR then disallowed the goal for offside due to his arm being in front of the defence, when he was pointing to where he wanted the ball to go. That is how ridiculous VAR is and what a ludicrous decision!

Klich skidded on the surface and went down with a hurt knee that brought the trainer on as Palace won a free kick in a good position outside the penalty area after a foul by Koch. Sadly for us the free kick went straight over the wall into the top left-hand corner under the crossbar to see us two goals down in the 23rd minute. Leeds then pulled a goal back within three minutes to give us a fighting chance when Bamford volleyed the ball past their keeper with three of their players around him in the penalty area. Leeds then had most of the play after scoring our goal. We won a corner, but Harrison's cross was headed away. Costa then scored an unlucky own goal after Palace suddenly attacked, but I thought he would be able to win the ball as they were running down the wing. With Meslier anticipating the cross he glanced to see who else was coming into the area, but the deflection went in at the near post and he was too late to get there. That meant Leeds were losing 3-1 at half-time when it could have been so different had our first goal been allowed to stand.

Raphinha came on for Costa at the start of the second half as Leeds tried to get back into the game. Struijk's header from a Harrison corner went wide then Palace had a shot from the edge of the area that went wide. Leeds then won another corner but sadly it did not amount to a good chance. A great break from Leeds saw Klich put a great ball out to Alioski on the left, who saw his shot tipped round the post by the keeper. Another attack saw Klich put a great cross from the byline across the box which Struijk headed down and Harrison shot straight at the keeper who saved it. Alioski then put a great ball across the area which was crying out for someone to smack it into the net, but it bypassed everyone.

Palace then upped their tempo after a good Leeds spell and won a corner. Leeds broke out of defence but then lost the ball and as Palace counter attacked, they put the ball across the box which found their player all on his own to slot the ball past Meslier for a fourth goal on the day. Although looking down and out, Leeds never gave up and suddenly Harrison put a great cross into the middle only for the ball to come off Bamford's shoulder and the chance went. Roberts replaced Struijk who I thought had done well. Once we were losing 4-1 it was painful to watch the rest of the game. Palace nearly got a fifth, but Meslier rose to the challenge and won the ball. Leeds won a free kick in a good position after Klich was brought down and Raphinha took it which was not far away from a goal.

After a great ball out to the wing, the ball came to Bamford who got into the penalty area and was brought down when their player stood on the back of his foot. Immediately we were told to play on but if there was a VAR decision, it was made in seconds and ignored. How could Leicester be given their penalty on Monday as their man was on the line with the ball outside the area and VAR decided it was a penalty minutes after the event? Personally, I cannot see the difference when Bamford's was actually in the area and not given. Sadly, it would not have made any difference as Leeds lost 4-1 for the second time in a week. It was another disappointing trip to London after all.

It would have been a long journey home after the loss, that is for sure. With the international break upon us once more, I would gladly kick those into touch for the disruption they are causing to the game in general. The other side of the coin is it gives us a chance to recuperate and hopefully have some of our injured and missing players ready for the next game after the break. There will be no easy games in this league, and I still prefer to see our attacking play although we can have all the possession in the world and not put any pressure on the opposition. We should try to shoot on sight rather than always taking that extra step and catch teams unawares. The opposition know they can let us attack and then catch us on the break, so we need to be able to shore up our midfield so that the defence is not overloaded and give Meslier more protection. Keep the faith.

LUFC – Marching on Together!

LEEDS UNITED V ARSENAL; 22 NOVEMBER 2020 AT ELLAND ROAD

With less than five weeks to go to Christmas, my Leeds United-themed Christmas tree is up. Don't forget to buy my latest book *Leeds Are Going to the Premier League! Leeds United Season 2019-20: Promotion in their Centenary Year!* for the Leeds fan in your life. Apart from spending time with my family, the greatest present would be to see Leeds fans back at Elland Road on Boxing Day. A nice touch from Leeds showed ball boy Elliott Metcalfe, who is suffering from cancer, being mascot for the day and leading the team out via an iPad. This may have been a contribution, but as the game kicked off, I suddenly felt really down as the tears started to flow.

Team: Meslier, Cooper, Ayling, Dallas (making his 200th appearance), Phillips (back from his shoulder injury), Raphinha (making his first home start), Bamford, Klich, Harrison, Koch, Alioski.
Subs: Rodrigo for Ayling (70), Poveda for Harrison (80).
Subs not used: Casilla, Costa, Roberts, Davis, Struijk.
Leeds drew the game 0-0 despite hitting the post and crossbar.
Attendance: Zero, behind closed doors.
Referee: Anthony Taylor.
Booked: Cooper, Dallas, Phillips.

Raphinha got in a good position to shoot after Leeds had to be on their toes to stop a couple of Arsenal attacks. After a lot of possession from Arsenal, it felt like it would be a tough game especially after they had a long-range shot which I thought had gone in, but it went wide. After a great run by Harrison and a perfect pass into the penalty area for Alioski to pass back to Bamford, his first time shot went straight to the keeper but there was not a lot of power in it. Dallas got booked when he rushed into a challenge with their player but replays from the opposite side of the pitch showed he got the ball first. Arsenal got a corner from the resulting free kick but did not do anything with it. Leeds had a couple of good moves but did not get the rub of the green with the final shots blocked. It looked heavy

going on the pitch too which was not helped by recent rainfalls, but I could not tell if it was still raining or not. Arsenal hit the top of the crossbar from a cross from the left of the Kop which looked as if it was going over, but the rebound was cleared away. Phillips slipped as he ran towards their player and brought him down for a free kick, but he did not get booked for it and luckily their shot went wide from it.

Another good move saw their player in a great position in our penalty area, but he mishit and shot wide. We started misplacing passes and putting pressure on ourselves which stood out for a while but then we overcame that. A great counter-attack saw Leeds race forward and Raphinha's shot went narrowly wide. It was good to see him not be scared to have a shot from a distance. Another move saw Leeds win a corner but sadly Bamford's volley, having done well to get in a position to have a go, was saved by their keeper. Another chance came to Dallas which went wide after some real persistence from Harrison down the wing towards the South Stand. Another great move saw Klich's shot go over the crossbar when it should have at least been on target. Ayling was the next one to have a shot go over from a free kick on the left when Alioski was brought down, before Arsenal had another attack with their final shot wide. After a lot of Leeds attacking, it looked like Arsenal had breached our defence before a counter-attack saw Leeds nearly through. Sadly, Bamford slipped as the pass came to him, but the whistle blew as Leeds went into the break on equal terms.

Arsenal brought a sub on at the start of the second half. An off-the-ball incident saw Alioski on the floor holding his face. Alioski had got the better of their player holding him off and he obviously did not like it. The referee had to look at the TV screen for VAR which showed Pépé headbutt Alioski who went down. There was no doubt in my mind that he had to be shown a red card and the referee agreed and sent him for an early bath. It was a stupid thing to do after approximately five minutes of play in the second half. With ten minutes gone Phillips pulled up holding his knee again. Arsenal made a change whilst Phillips was off the pitch as doubts about him continuing grew in my mind, but he did come back on. Our final crosses into the box were not getting to our players as Arsenal defended well. Arsenal counter-attacked with only Meslier to beat. Meslier came off his line and stood up to be counted and saved the shot putting the ball out for a corner.

I felt that maybe we should start to change things as we were getting caught out in defence by pushing up to the halfway line. As nobody was playing badly, I did not think Bielsa would change things as yet. I wanted us to pressure them, and we needed that final ball to get to our players in the penalty area. From another Leeds attack, a great shot from Dallas was saved by their keeper. The resulting corner saw Arsenal defend well but by lumping balls in there, we needed to find a way of getting better crosses into the penalty area. As I shouted foul throw by the Arsenal player, it was good to see the referee agreed with me as he gave the throw to Leeds. I found I was watching Phillips like a hawk to check he was not limping as a couple of times I was not too sure whether he was or not. Luckily, my fears looked to be ungrounded as he carried on playing. When it was said on the TV that their player was sent off for retaliation, I could not believe my ears. Alioski stood his ground as there was some pushing and shoving from both players and Pépé obviously could not take being stood up to.

As another attack saw Arsenal clearing the ball every time we got through, I was shouting for us to keep the ball on the floor as they were defending in numbers making it hard for us to get through. A bad pass from Raphinha saw Arsenal counter-attack us again and as Meslier went for the ball, Cooper took it from in front of him and made sure we cleared it. Another chance for Leeds saw a great pass back to Ayling who was unable to get the last touch of the ball. As it was, that became Ayling's last part of the game as he was then substituted. Dallas went to right-back and Rodrigo took over the number ten spot. After so much Leeds possession, a rare Arsenal attack saw Cooper push their player in the back to give a free kick away in a bad position. The resulting free kick went over the crossbar to my relief.

With 15 minutes of play left my cry was to keep fighting and never give up. Rodrigo hit a great shot from outside the area which was inches wide. Their player got the better of Phillips on the wing as they won a corner which meant I was starting to get nervous

although I had not been too bad until then. As Poveda was waiting to come on to the pitch as substitute, Rodrigo hit a great shot which came back off the crossbar. As Poveda replaced him, Harrison was seen to be limping as he went off. Suddenly Arsenal were through as Koch was beaten by a fantastic cross, but Cooper blocked the ball in the penalty area. As he fell the ball hit his elbow, but I was glad that the hand ball rules have been changed as it meant we played on. Arsenal were still defending in numbers, but Leeds then had a shot from Poveda saved by their keeper. It was starting to become a very frustrating game with the feeling that we were not going to break through their defence.

We had Meslier to thank after Arsenal were through again. We have got to be careful with the pushing up and getting caught out on the counter-attack. Cooper was booked for bringing their player down on the right. Poveda persisted in battling for the ball but was unlucky as the final ball to our player was short. The woodwork again saw Bamford very unlucky as his header hit the post after an excellent cross from Poveda. We need more of those crosses to put the opposition under pressure in my opinion. Klich then shot over after Poveda's shot was cleared as far as him. I thought Arsenal were time wasting in the final minutes after their player was fouled and their trainer came on to the pitch. On his way off the pitch their player was limping with the opposite foot that Alioski had stood on accidentally when he won a tackle. Phillips was booked for a foul too. Raphinha hit the post with a minute left, and I was positive that we would have sucked that ball into

the net from the Kop today had we been in attendance. The stats showed Leeds had 24 attempts on goal, wow, but sadly none of them ended up with a goal recorded. Leeds won a corner in the final minute of the game and as we went to take a short corner the whistle blew for full time.

With a no-score draw in the end, we got a point which was probably a good result for us after recent results went against us. After the whistle had blown, suddenly, their number three, Tierney, started being an arse and having a go at Alioski. As he did this more than once, it is a shame the referee did not send him off as really there was no need for it. After another international break has just ended with the potential for injuries to our players, I am glad we have a break from them too. We have a couple of tough away fixtures next with first Everton and then Chelsea. I feel we are playing well although not getting the goals we deserve but need to tighten up our defence, so we are not as exposed by a counter-attack. Keep fighting Leeds!

LUFC – Marching on Together!

EVERTON V LEEDS UNITED; 28 NOVEMBER 2020 AT GOODISON PARK

It was good hearing the news about the East Stand being renamed the Jack Charlton Stand this week. Big Jack played a total of 762 competitive appearances for Leeds United and we were the only club he played for, which was a fantastic achievement, and this is a well-deserved honour in his memory. The Calls in Leeds has now got a fantastic painting of Kalvin Phillips, Lucas Radebe and Albert Johanneson on a wall which is very impressive. Sad news was hearing one of our Whitby Whites fans who had travelled home and away for 50 years had died in tragic circumstances and young Louie had lost his battle with leukaemia. Recently when it was said that Louie did not have very long to live, he was FaceTimed at his bedside by members of the first team. My thoughts go out to all families and friends of both fans.

Team: Meslier, Ayling, Cooper, Alioski, Koch, Phillips, Harrison, Bamford, Raphinha, Klich, Dallas.
Subs: Costa for Harrison (81), Poveda for Raphinha (84), Rodrigo for Bamford (90).
Subs not used: Casilla, Struijk, Davis, Roberts.
Leeds won the game 1-0 with Raphinha scoring for Leeds (79).
Attendance: Zero, behind closed doors.
Referee: Chris Kavanagh.
Booked: Ayling, Cooper.

As Leeds kicked off, we were straight on the attack, and I thought we had won a corner in the first minute when Ayling got forward only for a goal kick to be given. There was a lively 20 minutes of football from both teams. A fantastic move from Leeds after excellent play by Raphinha saw him put a great pass across the box only for Harrison's shot to go narrowly wide. Everton attacked and with their man bearing down on him, Cooper let the ball go and their man on the wing passed the ball across to the same player in the middle. Meslier made a fantastic save from him and again quickly got to the rebound as Ayling ensured we cleared the ball. The play was end-to-end but Leeds were putting some good moves together. Suddenly, it looked like the game had turned on its head as Everton scored, but their player had strayed offside before smacking a great shot into the net from the byline. I could not believe VAR had to check it to be honest. That disallowed goal seemed to give Everton a bit of hope and Ayling was booked for shirt-pulling before their resulting free kick went over the crossbar. Leeds were unlucky not to score after their keeper made a fantastic save from a Raphinha header and then they kicked the ball off the line from Harrison's shot from the rebound. Bamford won Leeds a free kick, but we did not see their player get booked for shirt-pulling.

As Leeds continued to attack, three times Ayling passed the ball into the penalty area, but Everton stood firm blocking every attempt. Meslier saved another shot from Everton and then as Leeds counter-attacked, Everton were lucky not to concede a penalty for handball after Harrison's persistence in the penalty area saw the ball hit the hand of an Everton player. Meslier was in impressive form as he pushed the ball out for a corner after another attack from Everton. Again, it looked like Everton had taken the lead, but the linesman had put his flag up for offside. There was an Everton player in front of Meslier but well offside, so it was a correct decision. Meslier continued to keep us in the game by saving another shot. The pace had been relentless in the first half and just before the break we saw Harrison's header come back off the post with the keeper beaten and Bamford's shot from the rebound went wide. It did look like Ayling was coming up behind him and was in a better position to score, but you must take a chance when it is there. Klich had a great shot that just passed the wrong side of the post in injury time. It had been a good first half despite not making any chances count, having played some fantastic Bielsa-ball football. Just what I want to see.

The second half saw Everton have a good move but luckily Meslier put it round the post for a corner. As a Leeds move broke down with Bamford's shot blocked, Everton raced to the other end although they looked offside but put the chance wide. Leeds continued to attack with another great move but the final shot from Klich was well over the crossbar when he should have kept it down. Another chance saw us beat the defence, but Bamford's snapshot lifted too high and went over the top. A bad Meslier kick out from defence nearly saw us punished, but Meslier got back to keep the ball at the right side of the line despite his body going over it. Another great cross from Raphinha who had switched sides with Harrison saw no one there to put the ball into the net. The football was still end-to-end and some nice play ended after Bamford's pass to Harrison brought a save out of their keeper. A good move from Everton saw some good defending from Klich as he put a deflected shot out for a corner.

When Delph, an ex-Leeds player, came on for Everton, I had thought he looked familiar but could not say who he was. For me it is out of sight out of mind. I was expecting a great pass from Phillips to go wide but it went forwards to Harrison and we were unlucky that the final shot did not come off, but it was another good move. Keep fighting, Leeds, a goal will come. Raphinha after some good play in the penalty area was unlucky to see his shot blocked. Bamford then put the ball into the net, which was disallowed, but I thought the ball may have gone out before Alioski's cross. Replays showed Alioski had strayed offside. Everton won another corner as they made their second sub. Meslier then made another save and had to be quick to get to the rebound first.

We were starting to be put under pressure as I began to feel a little anxious that we needed to change things with 14 minutes left. As it was when no one was being brought on, I knew I had to trust Bielsa's judgement. Once again that proved right with a fantastic goal from Raphinha shortly after. He received the ball just outside the penalty area and when it looked like he was going to pass the ball, he changed his mind and sent a great shot through the defender's legs and past the keeper into the net. What a fantastic goal to put Leeds into the lead on the day.

We did not have long to see the game out now to get the three points. Harrison was seen limping down the touchline as he was replaced by Costa. Poveda was brought on for Raphinha and later with three minutes of injury time left to play, I was hopeful the result would go our way. Rodrigo was brought on for Bamford who was not happy to go off with a minute or so left. Phillips was fouled which saw their player booked at the death. Costa should have scored after great work from Poveda, but he took a second touch of the ball which saw their keeper block his shot when a first-time shot would have hit the back of the net.

Nevertheless, a great win and three points today as well as a fantastic team performance from Leeds United. Overall, the game itself was a good advert for football, especially for any neutrals. For me, when Raphinha's shot hit the back of the net I was dancing around the room as well of thousands of Leeds fans around the world no doubt. The only thing missing was seeing Leeds fans behind the goal celebrating the win. Next week sees another away game at Stamford Bridge against Chelsea. Just go out there and play football the way I want to see it and who knows what happens. The best form of defence is attack and this takes me back to the Revie days. As I have said before, if Bielsa can emulate Don Revie's team then we are in for a great future. We are not doing a bad job so far, are we?

LUFC – Marching on Together!

CHAPTER 4 – DECEMBER 2020

CHELSEA V LEEDS UNITED; 5 DECEMBER 2020
AT STAMFORD BRIDGE

Thank you, Kate and Rob, for buying my new book *Leeds Are Going to the Premier League!* There is still time to buy a last-minute Christmas present for the Leeds fan in your life either direct from my publisher or from Amazon.

With a busy week behind me, it has kept me away from things going on behind the scenes although I had heard there were doubts about Koch's fitness for the game. As it was, he was named on the team sheet.

Team: Meslier, Koch, Cooper, Ayling, Dallas, Phillips, Alioski, Bamford, Klich, Harrison, Raphinha.
Subs: Diego Llorente for Koch (9), Poveda for Harrison (57), Rodrigo for Alioski (69).
Subs not used: Casilla, Roberts, Costa, Struijk.
Leeds lost the game 3-1 with Bamford scoring an early goal for Leeds (4).
Attendance: 2,000 Chelsea fans allowed back in the ground for the first time since the last COVID lockdown, but no away fans.
Referee: Kevin Friend.
Booked: Raphinha, Llorente.

Our return to Stamford Bridge saw Bielsa up against Lampard. I admit I have not got fond thoughts of him but despite everything that happened in the play-offs against Derby in the second leg, I loved the 'stop crying Frank Lampard' song at the away leg.

The game kicked off at a cracking pace with Chelsea on the attack which saw Meslier save with his feet with the very first shot they had. Chelsea then came near with a header with only two minutes on the clock. The game turned on its head as Leeds counter-attacked which saw a great pass from Phillips on the wing to Bamford in the middle of the pitch. He ran through the defence, rounded the keeper, and struck a first-time shot into the net in the fourth minute! Get in Leeds, a great start!

Koch had already been fouled but then went down injured and had to go off in the ninth minute with Llorente coming on for his league debut. Immediately it looked like Chelsea had equalised from a corner but somehow the ball came out when it looked as if it had gone into the net. Replays showed their player stopped it going in, then Meslier saved it and the ball hit the crossbar and was then cleared but we survived. It did not take long to realise that this was going to be a tough game but then Leeds nearly scored a second goal.

Leeds played some great attacking football but Alioski's shot hit the post and came back out but the flag went up for offside so it would not have counted anyway. We then started to mess about at the back and although there was a bad pass out from Meslier, the defence were putting him under pressure. Don't do it, Leeds. Luckily for us the shot was wide. Some good work from Raphinha saw Bamford's shot saved by the keeper who looked unsighted, but there was not enough power in the shot to get past him. With that Chelsea went to the other end and scored to equalise just before the half hour mark. One of their players was injured in the build-up and then subbed.

A bad ball by Llorente across the box was won by Chelsea but somehow, we managed to clear the ball. They were a very fast team in attack, but we were giving them too much room on the wing as Cooper put the ball out for a corner. Meslier caught the ball well from the resulting header. Harrison then switched sides with Raphinha before a great tackle from Alioski set up an attack, but Raphinha's cross was cleared. Phillips's ball to Alioski was picked up by them to run at us again but we managed to get the ball back as three minutes' injury time was put up on the board. Harrison was struggling at times today with two men on him every time he got the ball. Llorente made an important tackle but then our attack broke down. Chelsea counter-attacked and had an open run down the wing but luckily for us the shot went wide.

As we came out for the second half, we had not made any changes to the team but to me we didn't start very well. We started to mess about at the back and looked hesitant and once again we were nearly punished for it. Raphinha stayed down when caught in the face although it did not look too bad contact. Meslier nearly had the ball taken off his toes as Leeds cleared the ball. Chelsea were continuing to be very quick on the attack and although I hate to say it, Lampard has got them playing football. Maybe it helped him by Chelsea having a transfer ban last season. There was some good defending from Cooper as he shielded the ball out for a goal kick. Another time as we headed the ball back to Meslier, he was going the opposite way and had to change direction and get back for the ball. Leeds saw Raphinha hit a great ball which was blocked and as the rebound came to him, he hit it over the crossbar, but it was a good attempt. Poveda then came on for Harrison after 57 minutes which was what I thought would happen. Meslier then made a fantastic double save from Chelsea before some great defending from Alioski saw him put the ball out for a corner. Unfortunately for us they scored from that, although it looked like Cooper was fouled just before it went into the net but only the goal for Chelsea was given.

As Chelsea came close after another attack, I knew we needed to make a change. I had already said that Alioski should come off for Rodrigo prior to Bielsa making the decision, showing we were on the same wavelength. Chelsea were closing us down well and continued to attack us with Meslier saving a long-range shot from them. Rodrigo started making a difference and was involved in a couple of good attacks before Bamford made a great tackle to win the ball back but got hurt in the process. Llorente kept sending long balls forward which gave Chelsea the impetus to attack as they won the ball every time. As I was critical of us messing about at the back, I suppose I cannot have it both ways. He was also booked for a foul on his debut.

Chelsea were a strong side and after winning the ball from Poveda made another attack but Meslier saved with his legs. Leeds managed to find a bit of space and after some great work by Poveda his shot was low and straight at the keeper, but it was a good move. He was fouled in the box in the build-up and the pundits were saying if he had gone down, we would have got a penalty. As Dallas slipped which meant he lost the ball, I could not help but think of the number of times we slip in comparison to other teams. Is it down to the boots our players wear as I cannot remember other teams slipping as much as we do on a regular basis? Deep into injury time, Chelsea counter-attacked and beat Dallas for pace down the wing and put the ball across for them to get a third goal. Raphinha too then found himself in the book for a foul.

Another game in London that went against us, but we never stopped trying and, on the day, Chelsea deserved their win. I will admit I had no idea that their win would take them to the top of the table tonight so I can't say they played well because they had their fans back! These things will happen, and it is another learning curve for us as I resigned myself to the defeat. On to the next game which sees us play West Ham next Friday evening at Elland Road.

LUFC – Marching on Together!

LEEDS UNITED V WEST HAM UNITED; 11 DECEMBER 2020 AT ELLAND ROAD

Sadly, with Leeds still being in Tier 3 for COVID-19, it meant no fans were allowed back into Elland Road. At the end of the game tonight, I felt so frustrated and would have coped so much better by being back at Elland Road. With the new floodlights now in the West Stand car park, hopefully it means my camera will cope better with photos at night games once we are allowed back. I was glad to hear that my new book *Leeds Are Going to the Premier League!* had arrived safely in Norway. I am looking forward to seeing photos from those fans who have already bought the book and those receiving it as a Christmas present.

This morning saw a Leeds United coffin being offered for sale on Instagram, although I was not aware of it until tonight. Should I be worried that my granddaughter Hannah and daughter Emily thought it would be ideal for me – although I did have a good laugh with them. Now I do like the idea of a Leeds United coffin, but I am not ready to meet my maker for a long while yet thank you.

Team: Meslier, Alioski, Cooper, Dallas, Phillips, Klich, Harrison, Raphinha, Rodrigo, Bamford, Ayling.

Subs: Shackleton for Alioski (45), Costa for Harrison (45), Roberts for Bamford (74).

Subs not used: Casilla, Hernández, Poveda, Struijk.

Leeds lost the game 2-1 with Klich scoring our goal, a penalty (6).

Attendance: Zero, behind closed doors.

Referee: Michael Oliver.

Booked: Alioski.

When Bielsa told the media on Wednesday what team he was going to use today, I thought it was a little bit too early to give the opposition that information. Did it come back to bite us on the backside tonight? Who knows? With injuries to both Koch (had surgery on his knee) and Llorente after the Chelsea game last week, this meant a change of formation for us. Dallas went to left-back and Ayling came in alongside Cooper in centre of defence with Alioski further up the pitch.

Leeds had a great start to the game with Cooper winning the ball and passing a great ball through for Bamford to run on to, who was brought down by the keeper and awarded a penalty. When Klich took the penalty, it was very tame and sent to the left of the goal as we were looking at it, where the keeper saved it. It was not the fact that the keeper saved it that I was berating Klich for, but there was no power in the shot. With that I was eating my words as VAR said the penalty had to be re-taken due to their keeper moving his feet off the line. To be honest, I did not notice anything at all, so it was a relief to get a second chance at it. This time Klich made no mistake as he sent a great shot into the bottom-right of the goal to give us a sixth minute lead.

Maybe the re-take wound West Ham up as they won the ball back attacking us with two on two and luckily Cooper recovered and put it out for a corner. West Ham had a great chance, but the header was straight at Meslier. Replays showed Phillips got in the way of it and took the sting out of the ball. They had another chance but this time it was Ayling who took the sting out of it. We were letting them into the game as West Ham had a good ten-minute spell. Leeds had a couple of attempts with Rodrigo's shot going wide after Alioski's cross then a good run from Raphinha, but there was not enough power on the shot which the keeper picked up easily. West Ham equalised from a corner in the 24th minute with a header that Meslier was unlucky not to get to as Dallas was kept down by their player. Leeds tried to get back into the game with a good attempt from Rodrigo although the ball was hit straight at their keeper. Another shot from West Ham went wide before Leeds won a corner. As I was saying what a waste of a corner as the ball went back nearly to the halfway line, the forward ball nearly came to Harrison in the box, but the ball just ran away in front of him. Alioski was booked before a couple more attempts from Leeds with a header from Bamford straight at the keeper and a nice shot from Ayling although it was an easy save for their keeper.

Bielsa made two subs at the start of the second half, bringing on Shackleton for Alioski and Costa for Harrison. I was happy to see Shackleton back as we needed a bit more in midfield and he could support Klich. A good move from Shackleton saw Bamford turn and shoot but it went wide. A good block by Ayling, although he did not know much about it, saw the ball go out for a corner. With their next one Meslier tipped the header over the crossbar. I found it frustrating as it felt that we were going back in defence a lot even though I knew we were trying to break West Ham down.

West Ham were still playing well and attacking us and came close again, but the ball went past the post. Phillips had a good shot put wide by West Ham then from a corner, there was a great shot from Klich saved by their keeper. It was a shame the ball did not deflect off Bamford and go in. Roberts was brought on to replace Bamford on 74 minutes who had gone down a few minutes earlier after a challenge. I was disappointed that we had not brought Hernández on earlier as I felt the game was crying out for a bit of flair from him. Benrahma to me was running their midfield. West Ham luckily put a shot wide when it looked like Cooper had decided to pull out of the tackle so as not to give away a penalty.

I was getting more and more frustrated as the game went on. There was a fantastic save made from Meslier after Leeds could not defend the set piece once again. A good pass from Rodrigo looked promising but Roberts could not get on the end of it. I was just feeling that the only winner of the game was going to be West Ham and with that they did indeed score a second goal with a header from the free kick. West Ham had a couple more chances with a fantastic save from Meslier from an overhead kick and they nearly got a third goal which bounced back off a post. After lots of West Ham pressure there was a corner for Leeds, but we were unlucky as the header from Rodrigo was straight at their keeper. At that moment I would have taken a draw, but it was not to be as Leeds lost the game 2-1. The second game in a row where Leeds had taken an early lead but ended up on the losing side.

It is certainly going to be a long tough season, but I found this defeat harder to take as it had been so frustrating to watch for me. We need that Elland Road crowd back there as the lads need us behind them. With another home game midweek against Newcastle and what would have been a return trip for us Leeds fans to Old Trafford next week, we really need some points in the bag very quickly. You know what to do Leeds!

LUFC – Marching on Together!

LEEDS UNITED V NEWCASTLE; 16 DECEMBER 2020 AT ELLAND ROAD

My message to Leeds before the game was keep fighting and never give up. We got our just rewards by doing that.

Team: Meslier, Cooper, Ayling, Alioski, Harrison, Klich, Phillips, Bamford, Rodrigo, Raphinha, Dallas.
Subs: Hernández for Rodrigo (82), Roberts for Bamford (84), Shackleton for Klich (89).
Subs not used: Casilla, Davis, Poveda, Struijk.
Leeds won the game 5-2 after going a goal down. Scorers: Bamford (35), Rodrigo (61), Dallas (82), Alioski (85) and Harrison (88).
Attendance: Zero, behind closed doors.
Referee: Simon Hooper.
Booked: Phillips, Klich, Raphinha.

Leeds were led out with another virtual mascot on an iPad, this time young Jude Hawkridge who is battling leukaemia. Hopefully, that and the win has given the young lad a boost, keep fighting.

The game kicked off with Leeds attacking the South Stand. Newcastle had a cross that went just over the crossbar. We won a corner, but it did not go well and ended with Newcastle getting a free kick. When the ball hit a Newcastle hand in the penalty area, I was not surprised to hear that it was a sensible ruling from the commentators. It always is when it is a handball in our favour and not against us! A shot from Rodrigo was hit wrong and went over the top. The pitch was cutting up very quickly especially after the recent heavy rainfall again. It did not get re-laid in the summer due to lack of time with COVID, but the groundsman does a great job under the circumstances.

I was starting to get frustrated very early on by the sloppy passing and then told myself to stop it as Leeds will grow into the game. I thought we were very unlucky with a great pass across the box which Klich just missed, but the flag was up so it would not have counted. We had had 74 per cent possession at this point but need to make sure goals come from it. Good work from Alioski and Harrison saw Leeds win a corner. Leeds were very unlucky not to take the lead with a great header from Cooper which was saved by their keeper. When the linesman put his flag up for offside again, I realised we were going to have to watch our line as I told him to stick the flag where the sun doesn't shine. A back pass to Meslier was too close for comfort as it was very close to their player too. We had another great move, but Harrison's ball was put across the front of goal but not near enough our players as Leeds were starting to take charge of the game. Raphinha did some great work in the penalty area but then hit a wild shot wide. As a shot from Klich went over the bar but not by much. My shout was keep it down Leeds and let's get a hatful please. Newcastle then intercepted the ball and looked dangerous with the resulting shot pushed out by Meslier and eventually to safety. As I was saying out loud that it was important that Newcastle do not get anything, they damn well scored with 26 minutes on the clock. Their cross saw a header across to the back post where their player got behind Alioski and slammed the ball into the net.

Harrison got smacked in the nose and mouth in the run-up to their goal, although I never saw what happened, but he had to change his shirt as he was bleeding. I said we were going to win now as the pressure was off us again, so we had no need to fear them. Raphinha was playing really well as the keeper saved a shot from him. He then sent a great cross to Rodrigo which came off the bar with the rebound headed into the net by Bamford to equalise. That was a vital goal to get us back on equal terms before half-time. Klich was booked for a challenge as I was asking why was it a booking? Half-time saw us going into the break on equal terms.

At the start of the second half Phillips was the next one to be booked for an innocuous challenge. A bad kick out from Meslier put our player into trouble as Newcastle attacked but Klich stopped it going out for a corner. A Leeds attack ended with a shot from Raphinha as replays were shown that our breakaway began after a strong challenge by Cooper in our area. The referee was happy with his decision not to give a penalty to Newcastle. Alioski's cross was straight to their keeper, he went on a good run after receiving Harrison's cross. A good pass from Rodrigo saw some good work from Bamford in the area who turned and shot, but the ball lacked power and was easily saved by the keeper. I noticed Leeds were now hitting the ball with more conviction and power. A fantastic ball from Rodrigo was sent to Harrison on the left who did brilliantly to get the ball and he sent a great ball over for Rodrigo to head into the net on 61 minutes to put Leeds back into the lead.

Leeds continued to attack with a great header to Bamford and the keeper saved a low shot. From the resulting corner, which was terrible, Newcastle counter-attacked which brought a brilliant tip over the crossbar by Meslier. Sadly, the corner saw their player rise above everyone to head the ball into the net with Meslier unsighted but still did his best to keep it out, having kept our lead for three minutes. As Newcastle threatened with another breakaway from a Leeds corner, Raphinha found himself in the book having stopped the attack.

Some good work from Bamford in the penalty area saw the ball just in front of our players as Newcastle cleared it. Another great attack from Leeds saw an excellent cross from Klich across the box to the far side where Dallas headed in for a third goal. Newcastle had just made their third sub and I hoped they were getting tired. With some of their players not training due to COVID reasons I had no idea if that had impacted on any who were playing today or not.

With Newcastle attacking once again, we saw some good back tracking from Bamford to win the ball back. As Hernández was getting ready to come on, Bamford was fouled but play carried on. Rodrigo went off for Hernández before Roberts came on for Bamford. A fantastic counter-attack from Leeds, after a great run from Raphinha, saw Alioski score to make it 4-2 to Leeds. Leeds players were queuing up to score which was great to see. Shortly afterwards we had another break away and as I was telling Harrison to pass, he sent a fantastic long range shot over the keeper for a fifth goal to make it 5-2 on the day. That's it, game over! Shackleton replaced Klich for the final few minutes as Leeds saw the game out. Raphinha was man of the match for me but as it was, any number of players could have got that today.

That win will breed confidence and I am glad they listened to my team talk before the game lol! Just what was needed before going across the Pennines to that team that play in that horrid colour red at the weekend. Just go out there and do us proud Leeds and keep fighting!

LUFC – Marching on Together!

MAN UTD V LEEDS UNITED; 20 DECEMBER 2020 AT OLD TRAFFORD

It was nice to see that my new book *Leeds Are Going to the Premier League!* made its appearance at Elland Road before I did. Thank you to Phil 'Thumbs Up' Cresswell who took his into the ground and was a good luck charm against Newcastle. Thank you also to Matt Wainwright and Robbie, Oliver and Eli who showcased the book outside the ground. I do miss going there.

I attended my first live football game yesterday since the Huddersfield home game in March, watching my granddaughter, Laura. It shows old habits die hard as I got carried away at one time and automatically shouted come on Leeds.

Team: Meslier, Cooper, Alioski, Ayling, Harrison, Bamford, Klich, Phillips, Rodrigo, Raphinha, Dallas.
Subs: Struijk for Phillips (45), Shackleton for Klich (45), Davis for Cooper (72).
Subs not used: Casilla, Poveda, Casey, Roberts, Hernández, Costa.
Leeds lost the game 6-2 after going down to a quick succession of goals but scored two goals with Cooper (42) and Dallas with a cracker (73) being the Leeds scorers.
Attendance: Zero, behind closed doors.
Referee: Anthony Taylor.

Leeds got off to the worst start ever, being three goals down within the first 20 minutes. Obviously, man u had raised their game. With one they ran through the middle and looked to catch us unawares. Bamford had a great chance, but it went wide. It was good to get a chance to give us hope that we were not out of the game as I was still looking for a draw at this point. Never give up fighting and still believe, Leeds. A draw would be a good result and we can get back in this game although it would not be easy. There was some good defending by Cooper as they attacked us again.

It seemed to me that the crowd noise had been upped as we do not normally hear it so loud. Commentators saying that our rivalry only started when Cantona was transferred to them made me laugh out loud. They also said that there may have been some before that, showing how silly and pathetic the discussion was as they have not got a clue. My experiences as a fan started in the early 1970s but fans who went to away games earlier than I did, had plenty of stories to tell of troubles they endured from their fans before ours started fighting back. The commentators also said that it was horrible that Leeds fans used to congregate outside their hotel when we played them. Poor souls, I do feel sorry for them, not! Surely that cannot be any worse than having sleep disturbed by your children as young babies, six years' worth in my case.

Cooper made another important interception. They were making sure we did not have the time to settle as Alioski gave a free kick away when he was nearly on Rashford's back marking him close. With an unchanged team, maybe we needed different tactics to get on top of them especially as we were up against a ten-man defence. Bamford scored but had strayed offside which would have got us back into this game. Instead, they got their third from their goal kick. Bamford was unlucky with a header after a great Klich cross. Believe, lads, was my cry as we continued to attack and got another corner. This was not a good one from Raphinha although it ended when the keeper saved with his feet, but it turned out Harrison was offside so it wouldn't have counted. man u won a corner and scored a fourth which Phillips should have defended better than he did.

If we had been at the ground some fans would have been clamouring to go to the pub but as a glutton for punishment, I would have stayed until the bitter end regardless. Leeds fans would have made our own entertainment; we're going to win 5-4! As it was, I was resigned to an even bigger defeat as Meslier saved when it looked like they were going to score a fifth goal, but the flag was also up for offside. Leeds still had not given up and Cooper pulled a goal back when he headed one home from a better corner from Raphinha in the 42nd minute. Meslier was forced to make another save before the break.

Leeds made a double substitution with both Struijk and Shackleton coming on for the second half with Klich and Phillips off. I am not sure if it were to do with them both being on four yellow cards or not but at times Phillips did look ineffective as the game passed him by. man u had another good chance just after the restart but put it wide. My hopes were raised when I thought we had scored a second goal after Raphinha and Bamford combined but it went out for a corner. Just after that the referee booked James for diving when I thought he had given a penalty. Leeds were still attacking and won another corner, but they broke out from our corner which ended with Shackleton blocking the ball. Back to Leeds on the attack and a shot from Raphinha was put around the post from the keeper. Once again man u broke away from our corner and with the ball running for them, they got a fifth goal that went through Meslier's legs. He had been left wide open so many times today that I could not apportion any blame to him. Cooper was injured but came back on to the pitch before man u were awarded a penalty after Struijk's tackle. At this point I knew we were not going to win 5-4 lol. Again, an idiotic commentator was saying Leeds fans would be glad not to be there. We support the team win, lose or draw and I would much rather be at the game watching it live in the ground than on TV, however welcome my log burner was.

Davis came on to replace Cooper who went off injured with his knee again by the look of it. Meslier saved another chance with his legs before a fantastic goal from Dallas made it 6-2. Leeds were winning plenty of corners today which will do us good as practice makes perfect. From one we had two players Struijk and Bamford down. Again, we had to thank Meslier for a double save to deny them a seventh. He was called into action again with another save off his knee and saving a header on his line. They won the ball from his throw out as we were not watching it and were too slow to react and they could have had a seventh but won a corner instead. After a good attacking move Harrison put the ball wide when in a good position.

It was hard to believe the score line when we kept attacking but it made it easier to forget we were losing. As it was, we were well beaten on the day in a game with end-to-end football that was a good advert for football itself and I will always be proud to be a Leeds United supporter.

As I finish my blog today, yesterday's government news re Christmas had me sobbing for hours I am not ashamed to say, as this is my favourite time of the year. Whatever anyone does, stay safe and healthy, but be happy.

LUFC – Marching on Together!

LEEDS UNITED V BURNLEY; 27 DECEMBER 2020 AT ELLAND ROAD

I hope everyone managed to have a good Christmas despite the challenging circumstances we all find ourselves under. My grandson Freddie now fits properly into this season's Leeds kit after he was born nine weeks prematurely. He is pictured with his Leeds football that he got for Christmas with a set of little goals. Simply perfect for someone born to be Leeds. Thank you to Andy Epp for sharing his photo with my new book *Leeds Are Going to the Premier League!* and Matt and Jack Brown who were delighted to receive their book showing

the foreword that they did for it. For all those who found the book amongst their Christmas presents this year, enjoy the read and thank you once again to everyone for your continued support which is greatly appreciated.

I finally managed to share on my website part of the Marcelo Bielsa documentary recorded by France TV in July which stars me, Adam Pope and Phil Hay. Sadly, due to copyright issues I was not able to share the whole documentary but a big thank you goes to Adam Pope for giving me something to share with everyone. Most of the documentary is in French apart from our pieces. I also recently found another of my cassettes of the Kop/Gelderd End singing from the Derby game on 6 April 1974 when I took my cassette recorder on to the Kop. I thought I must have mistakenly given that to Mick Hewitt when I sold a lot of my things to him after I moved to a new house 15+ years ago so was thrilled to find it. I will post that as soon as I can but listening to it all last night, brought back so many memories as Leeds went on to win the First Division as champions a few weeks later. I had been so scared to play it in case it snapped but hopefully I have found a way to get a copy of it to share.

Thank you to the Leeds United Supporters' Club Johannesburg branch for letting me share their photo of them watching the Burnley game today.

Team: Meslier, Ayling, Struijk, Alioski, Bamford, Rodrigo, Raphinha, Klich, Harrison, Phillips, Dallas.

Subs: Hernández for Rodrigo (59), Shackleton for Klich (66), Poveda for Raphinha (70).
Subs not used: Casilla, Davis, Costa, Roberts, Casey, Jenkins.
Leeds won the game 1-0 with a Bamford penalty (5).
Attendance: Zero, behind closed doors.
Referee: Robert Jones.

Bielsa had only made one change to the team due to Cooper's injury but looked to have changed our formation as we set off with three centre-halves with Phillips in the middle. We started off playing deep and messing about with our passing which ended with a Burnley corner. It was good to see we had a player on each post with reminisces of the Revie years for me. Leeds had a great attack which saw Ayling send a long forward pass that beat the defence. Bamford kept on running and was then brought down by the keeper to give Leeds a penalty. Bamford himself took a great penalty that sent him into double figures for goals scored, that put Leeds into the lead after five minutes.

A brilliant ball from Raphinha to Alioski in the penalty area should have ended better but the shot was poor. Meslier punched the ball out after a free kick was given for a Dallas push. Leeds had another good move with a shot from Rodrigo, but it lacked power and the keeper saved although he seemed to fumble the save. Another attack saw a Raphinha header going over the top, but the flag was up for offside. Burnley were given a free kick and scored from it. Meslier went for the ball, collided with their player and they scored from there despite the efforts of Ayling on the line, but it was then disallowed for a foul on our keeper. The commentators were ranting that it was a good goal but for once the decision went our way, so we were still leading after 19 minutes. Burnley were making it difficult for us to come forward as we kept passing the ball across the back four when all I wanted was for us to pass forwards to stop putting pressure on ourselves. Bamford won a corner and from a second corner their keeper tipped the ball over the top from Klich's shot. There was some nice play from Dallas as he shielded the ball to win it back. Klich had a shot that was way over the top of the goal, but it was worth a try as being unpredictable can work in our favour. I found myself kicking every ball desperate for us to not give Burnley anything at all. The referee gave Leeds a free kick after Rodrigo was fouled which earned their man a booking.

Another chance for Leeds was kicked off the line after some excellent play from Raphinha from a Harrison cross. At this moment of the game, on 32 minutes, Leeds had 70 per cent of the play. It looked like Wood, ex-Leeds, would score, but Ayling did enough to put him off with Meslier beaten. Some sloppy passing from Leeds was letting Burnley into the game. A Burnley corner saw Harrison and Raphinha on the line again, as Burnley were going mad shouting for another corner, but the referee gave a goal kick.

For all their shouting the referee got it spot on as the ball had indeed deflected but had come off their own player. Ayling won a free kick after being pushed off the ball by Wood which was another correct decision. Another great move resulted in a shot from Raphinha that was saved by the keeper. The nerves were certainly kicking in for me today as it was so important that we got three points after seeing that Arsenal had moved above us, putting us into 15th place which put me into an anxious mood. I told myself that we were playing well and would be fine.

Their player Barnes was moaning that he had been fouled but replays showed him pulling Struijk's shirt and keeping hold of his leg, silly man. Another great move saw Rodrigo recover to put the ball out wide to Harrison and then got on the end of the cross himself but sadly headed the ball wide. A shame really, as that would have been a great goal, but Leeds went into the break 1-0 in the lead thanks to the Bamford penalty.

As we kicked off towards the Kop at the start of the second half, I was willing Leeds on. We straight away started playing about at the back again which caused mistakes and put us under pressure. A good break out from Phillips saw a bad pass forwards that Burnley capitalised on to set up another attack. Some good defending from Phillips with a vital header saw him put the ball out. More good defending from Ayling saw Burnley get penalised for offside thankfully. I thought it was a tight decision but my husband disagreed with me so I reckoned it must be down to the angle of the ball as I sat to the side of the TV screen. Raphinha was unlucky when his shot was blocked as Burnley came away with the ball, but Harrison chased it down. This game looked rife for Hernández to come on at some point.

Meslier saved a couple of shots in near succession as Burnley had most of the attacking play at the start of the second half. We seemed to be bypassing midfield at this point as I thought we needed to change things as I did not want Burnley to score and get back into the game before we changed it. As it was, Hernández was already on his feet ready to come on in place of Rodrigo. Leeds were still having to do a lot of defending as Phillips got in front of Wood and put the ball out for a corner. We were putting ourselves under pressure with bad passing but the ball was running for Burnley. Playing out from the back is hard now but we need to back each other up. Every time we kick it out long, Burnley win it anyway so there is no happy medium at this moment. Leeds had a great move which really should have ended in a goal with Dallas in so much space, but his final shot was too high. Shackleton then came on for Klich.

Struijk was unlucky when the ball went out for a corner as he was shielding it when the ball rebounded off his leg. Luckily from the corner, Meslier caught the ball at the second attempt, but a free kick was given anyway. Raphinha made way for Poveda with 20 minutes left although I thought it would be Harrison going off, as Raphinha was making

it hard for Taylor down that side. Suddenly Leeds came forward with a counter-attack and a great run from Hernández saw their keeper put the ball round the post to prevent a second goal. Burnley were not giving up as their shot brought an excellent save from Meslier. Phillips was in the thick of it again, putting a header out from another corner as Burnley decided to make a double substitution. It felt like every minute to the final whistle was dragging in what seemed an awfully long game with just over 15 minutes left to play.

A Leeds attack broke down after Dallas should have hit a first-time cross but took a second touch of the ball. Struijk was on the floor but if was funny seeing him get up and come away with the ball. Burnley had more possession and chances so far without scoring, but I was hoping that we would come into the game in the last few minutes to get a second goal to seal the victory. Westwood was then booked for Burnley after a foul was given against him. Leeds got forward once more and were unlucky that the ball was whipped off Leeds toes in the penalty area before Bamford reached Hernández's pass. Burnley had another chance that went over the crossbar with Ayling putting him off. Another Leeds attack broke down after an excellent ball from Hernández to Harrison saw the final ball not reach Bamford.

Burnley were looking dangerous, and they won another corner as I was shouting for Leeds to clear it. Meslier punched the ball away then Burnley came back at us when Taylor got past Poveda, but Leeds managed to clear it. Meslier made another good save when he palmed the ball away from a corner. There was some great defending from Struijk, Phillips and Meslier but then the flag went up for offside giving us some respite. Barnes pushed Hernández over and was then booked for mouthing off about it. Good, as I hate mouthy players and he deserved to go in the book so well done referee.

With three minutes of injury time put up we faced a final onslaught as Ayling put the ball out for another corner to Burnley. As I was just wondering who the player in blue was, I suddenly realised it was their keeper. I would have loved a counter-attack at that time but sadly we did not get the opportunity. Phillips tried to stop the ball going out for a corner, but they ended up with a free kick instead with Meslier tipping the resulting free kick over the top. As Alioski came away with the ball the whistle blew for full time. Thank goodness for that and what a relief, as I did not want Burnley to score at all. However tight and desperate it was at times, three points are all that matters. This was one of those very nervous games where I was desperate for the win today which we got, but we also saw some great defending today so well done lads. Grinding out results are the signs of a good team. The win got us up the table to 11th and ready for our next battle on Tuesday at West Bromwich Albion.

LUFC – Marching on Together!

WEST BROMWICH ALBION V LEEDS UNITED; 29 DECEMBER 2020 AT THE HAWTHORNS

After being out for most of the afternoon I thought I had better check the kick-off time for the game as I had assumed it was 8pm. Mm, it is a good job I did otherwise I'd have missed a one-sided game with Leeds hammering WBA 5-0.

Team: Meslier, Ayling, Alioski, Dallas, Bamford, Klich, Rodrigo, Raphinha, Harrison, Struijk, Phillips.
Subs: Shackleton for Klich (58), Hernández for Rodrigo (70), Costa for Raphinha (81).
Subs not used: Casilla, Roberts, Davis, Jenkins, Casey, Poveda.
Leeds won the game 5-0 with an own goal by Sawyers (9), Alioski (31), Harrison (36), Rodrigo (40) and Raphinha (72) being the scorers of our goals.
Attendance: Zero, behind closed doors.
Referee: Lee Mason.
Booked: Alioski.

After the tense game against Burnley, one of my comments to others was that grinding out results shows we are a good team. Having had the privilege of watching the great Don Revie side, many times we had to do the same to get the points.

A fantastic cross from Rodrigo across the box saw no one far enough up the pitch to knock it into the net. The game turned on its head with a spectacular own goal nine minutes into the game when a long back pass was put straight into the goal with the keeper out of the goalmouth. That was just the start we needed. Leeds continued to attack and a through ball from Klich didn't get to our man but maybe he'd have been better having a go himself as a gap had opened up in front of him. WBA had a rare attack, but we had great back up from Dallas who put the ball out for a corner to them after taking the ball off their toes in the penalty area. A good shot from long range by Phillips was saved by their keeper. Dallas with a good bit of play down the wing saw the final cross blocked. Bamford passed the ball to Harrison who beat their man but sent a shot wide. It is always worth trying a shot but also a chip to one of our two players steaming in who were in a better position may have resulted in a goal.

As it was, we did not have long to wait for a second goal with a great cross from Raphinha over to Alioski who went on to smack a fantastic strike into the net to double our lead on 31 minutes. Leeds were now on a roll and a fantastic goal from Harrison made it three five minutes later. I thought Alioski looked like he had blood around his mouth before realising he was bleeding from his nose and had to go off to get a clean shirt and get seen to. I had not seen anything happen so hopefully someone will enlighten me in due course. Things were happening thick and fast as Leeds got a fourth with a deflected Rodrigo goal on 40 minutes. Wow, fantastic Leeds as the game was very one-sided, we were playing so well, and it was well deserved. Just after that Alioski was booked when diving in on their player. I wondered if that was a bit of retaliation and maybe he was the one who did something to him? Just before the break a Raphinha shot was pushed out by the keeper, just missing Harrison as they cleared the ball. A 4-0 score line at half-time showed how dominant Leeds had been. It was too much for Sam Allardyce who had only just taken over as manager, as he went down the tunnel before the whistle blew.

At the start of the second half there should have been a booking for a foul on the back of Raphinha's calf, but WBA got away with it. They came out with a bit more fight in them and won a corner but from that, Leeds won a free kick with a blatant push on Harrison. As the commentators were wondering if Leeds would still push for further goals, I knew the answer would be yes and the best form of defence is attack. A good run forwards saw Bamford's shot deflected for a corner, but this was cleared by WBA. It was quite funny seeing their player fall and sit on the ball when trying to attack as Leeds came away with the ball. As I shouted keep the comedy act up it did not quite work out that way. As we played out from the box

the back pass to Meslier put him under pressure and he passed a short ball out to our player that WBA got to first. As their player took the ball forward Meslier made a first save, then a second one, as we cleared the ball. Klich was down getting treatment and then went off with Shackleton brought on as a substitute.

There was some good defending from Rodrigo before WBA got another corner. This time Leeds broke away putting pressure on WBA before Hernández replaced Rodrigo. I was a little mystified when WBA had a throw in as I thought Meslier with plenty of time and space around him was going to pick the ball up. Suddenly he kicked it out for another throw in. That got me thinking, was he not allowed to pick the ball up from a throw in, did he get confused or did I miss a back pass? As far as I was concerned the keeper could pick the ball up unless there has been a rule change, I was not aware of? It did not really matter though because shortly afterwards, Raphinha made it five with a fantastic run down the wing and then across the box with a sweetly struck strike into the top left-hand corner of the goal.

Leeds were still looking to attack and a great ball from Hernández through to Dallas saw Leeds win a corner. Ayling was unlucky as he shot over the bar from the corner. Another good run this time from Alioski saw him pass to Harrison and his cross saw a great shot from Bamford hit their player and go out for a corner. Bamford, despite not being one of the scorers today, lost the ball but then fought and won it back but there was a WBA player down so Leeds put the ball out so he could receive treatment. Raphinha was replaced by Costa, but the former was extremely disappointed not to be staying on the pitch. A great cross from Harrison evaded everyone and was just out of reach of Struijk coming in at the far post trying to get to the ball. A bad pass from Hernández gave WBA a chance but offered no threat as their shot went way over the top of the goal. A couple more Leeds attacks saw firstly a good run from Ayling, but the final ball was cleared and then some good play between Dallas and Hernández.

There were only two minutes of injury time on the clock which surprised me but then I thought the referee would not want to prolong the agony for WBA. As Leeds started going backwards towards our goal, I was shouting do not go back we want six, as the whistle went for full time. What a result Leeds, thoroughly deserved and giving us another three points.

When this year started, I was glad to see the back of 2019 when my husband had a battle with cancer and my grandson Freddie was born 9 weeks prematurely. This was an incredibly stressful time for us as a family. As the year draws to a close and I reflect on 2020, little did I know this year was going to see Leeds United promoted back to the Premier League and we as fans were not allowed to be there in person to witness it. The COVID-19 pandemic has meant an incredibly challenging time for everyone, and I really hope that we can get back to some normality sooner rather than later. Leeds United lost three of our legends in Norman Hunter, Trevor Cherry and big Jack Charlton as well as many Leeds United fans throughout the year with some not even knowing we had achieved our dream of promotion. My thoughts go out to family and friends of all those who died.

Going forward into 2021, I really thought our 2 January trip to Spurs would see away fans back at games as I was looking forward to going to a new ground. Obviously, that will not happen, and neither will the visit to Crawley too in the FA Cup the week after. I cannot wait to be amongst our fans again and want to wish you all a Happy New Year and a better year in 2021.

LUFC – Marching on Together!

CHAPTER 5 – JANUARY 2021

TOTTENHAM HOTSPUR V LEEDS UNITED; 2 JANUARY 2021 AT THE TOTTENHAM HOTSPUR STADIUM

Here is to 2021 showing some light at the end of that awfully long dark tunnel. Today, I was looking forward to visiting a new ground but sadly we were still seeing games behind closed doors. Although I have been to White Hart Lane, their previous stadium, many times before, this would have been the first visit for me as well as other Leeds fans. As it was, sat at home with the log fire burning and the snow falling, at least we will not be battling the weather today.

Team: Meslier, Alioski, Ayling, Harrison, Rodrigo, Raphinha, Klich, Phillips, Dallas, Bamford, Struijk.
Subs: Poveda for Harrison (61), Shackleton for Alioski (64), Hernández for Rodrigo (65).
Subs not used: Casilla, Costa, Cresswell, Huggins, Casey, Jenkins.
Leeds lost the game 3-0; a penalty awarded to Spurs on 29 minutes changed the game.
Attendance: Zero, behind closed doors.
Referee: David Coote.
Booked: Phillips.

With the cameras being so far from the pitch I should have put my glasses on to watch them. Leeds made a good move which saw Alioski shoot into the side-netting which was a good chance. For the first seven minutes of the game, Leeds had a lot of possession and were going forward. Another good move out of defence saw Bamford unlucky with a chance. Meslier had to come out quick to claim the ball at the edge of the area as Spurs looked to be biding their time and come at us down the centre of the pitch. At the other end Bamford was being crowded out with four Spurs players around him at one time. I kept thinking it was a shame the early chance for Alioski did not come off.

Spurs shot over the bar when we could not clear the ball and it kept lingering benefitting Spurs and just after that Meslier made a save to keep them out. The referee played advantage after a foul and the final header from Bamford went over the bar, but it had been a good chance. A ball out from Meslier down the centre of the pitch to our man was picked up by Spurs instead who ran forward and got a penalty when Alioski brought their man down on the line. The ball should have gone to the right rather than the centre in my opinion, but they may have still won the ball. As that decision went against the run of play, to me it changed the game for us. They scored from the penalty which then gave them hope as Leeds relied on good defending to stop them getting a further goal.

Leeds were trying to get back into the game, taking a free kick quickly. Bamford did well to get it through their players as Spurs kicked the ball away just in front of their keeper for a throw-in for Leeds. Another good move saw Klich send a great pass through to Raphinha who found his shot saved by the keeper. The game was being played at a fast pace as Spurs counter-attacked and got in a dangerous position but luckily for us their shot went over the bar. There was some good defending from Ayling but with Leeds battling and still attacking, we got forward. Bamford chipped the ball into their penalty area, but there was no one close enough behind him to hit the ball into the net from a great position. Another fantastic move from Leeds ended with a great shot from Harrison that was just over the bar but deserved a goal. Nice play from Bamford on the edge of the box saw him wait ready to pass to two or three of our players, but a path opened for him, and the keeper saved his shot. Sadly, for us we took our eyes off the ball as Spurs counter-attacked with a long kick from their keeper. We managed to win the ball, but Spurs persistence saw them win it back and put a cross over that saw their player steal in between Dallas and Ayling to score a second goal just before half-time. That London hoodoo strikes again. As we were losing 2-0 at half-time, I would be happy to get a draw out of the game at least.

I was expecting changes for the start of the second half as I thought Phillips had been quiet in the first half, but Bielsa did not make any. As we started well with a good cross that was headed away, my initial thoughts were maybe Bielsa was right not making any changes as I shouted, 'Come on Leeds'. With that, a Spurs counter-attack saw the ball running for them after a quick free kick which saw a brilliant save from Meslier which rebounded around the post. Sadly, they got a third goal from the corner. Their player managed to head the ball when surrounded by our players and Meslier was very unlucky, stopping the ball just over the line when he tried keeping it out. Bielsa lost his balance at the side of the pitch as he was shouting out orders to the team. The penalty changed the game, but we needed to change our formation now. We were losing the ball in midfield which was the main issue for me, and we needed to change things. If Bielsa turned out to be right and we got back to 3-3 then I would eat my words.

As it was Bielsa did make changes with Poveda coming on for Harrison. Leeds were still attacking but Spurs were crowding us out in the penalty area before counter-attacking us again, which saw some good defending from Ayling and then another great save by Meslier. With Shackleton replacing Alioski and then a minute later Hernández on for Rodrigo, Leeds would continue to attack. When some Leeds attacking broke down, we had to be thankful for Meslier in goal making the save. Spurs were not giving us any space and the thing I found frustrating was no clear chances for us. As Spurs broke out from defence, they shot from the halfway line, but Meslier raced back in his goal as the ball went over. I was desperate for a goal to go in to give us hope as Leeds won two corners in quick succession

after good play from Hernández. A Raphinha shot was saved by their keeper in the 80th minute as Leeds tried getting closer to scoring. A great cross from Klich was just too far in front for Raphinha to get on the end of.

Most of the attacking was by Leeds now as they defended well from Spurs counter-attacks. A Bamford header was easily saved by their keeper, then Dallas was down getting treatment at one time but carried on playing afterwards. Phillips found himself in the book which means he is suspended for Crawley now after getting five bookings. To be honest it is good timing although I do not think he played well today, maybe he was shackled too much. Doherty was sent off for a foul on Hernández in injury time when the late tackle caught him on his instep. It is a shame this happened so late in the game that we could have used to our advantage although I would not have wished the tackle on Hernández. As the whistle blew for full time with Leeds losing 3-0, my mantra was, 'If at first you don't succeed, try, try, try again'. We will get there Leeds, but it will take time. I would much rather see our attacking play than spend 90 minutes passing the ball across the back four and never getting out of our half as we have done in the past. We win some and we lose some comes to mind.

On to Crawley in the FA Cup which would have been another new ground for me had we been allowed to be there. As someone posted on social media this week, we need to put a strong team out for the game, without those nearing suspension or battling injuries and go for it with some youngsters involved. I totally agree; the FA Cup is still dear to my heart with my favourite ever game seeing Billy Bremner lift the cup at Wembley from Her Majesty the Queen in 1972.

LUFC – Marching on Together!

CRAWLEY V LEEDS UNITED; FA CUP THIRD ROUND, 10 JANUARY 2021 AT THE PEOPLE'S PENSION STADIUM

After the recent further lockdown measures were announced which sent me once again into a downward spiral with plenty of tears, I know I am not the only one. To all of you out there who are struggling, I know I rely on family, friends, and my Leeds United family to talk about things and help me through. Please do the same as we are all in this and can pull through together.

Team: Casilla, Cooper, Davis, Struijk, Phillips, Costa, Poveda, Hernández, Shackleton, Alioski, Rodrigo.
Subs: Casey for Cooper (45), Jenkins for Struijk (45), Harrison for Rodrigo (45), Raphinha for Davis (58), Greenwood for Poveda (58).
Subs not used: Caprile, Huggins.
Leeds lost the game 3-0.
Attendance: Zero, behind closed doors.
Referee: Peter Bankes.
Booked: Phillips

From the start Crawley were looking to attack us as much as possible and forced two early corners. A great ball from Poveda to Rodrigo saw him stretch for the ball in their penalty area. Maybe it would still have been in front of him and out of reach, but a flying header may have been a better option, but it was a good move though. We saw some nifty footwork from Costa, and I am hoping the run-out today will start to give him confidence again, as he hasn't done so well for me when coming on as sub recently.

Crawley saw a deflected shot easily saved by Casilla. Leeds then had a couple of good chances and with one, a Poveda shot was saved by their keeper's feet. There were a few good moves from both sides that did not come to anything. There were two great balls sent through at different times that were really close to Shackleton, but he could not get on the end of them. We saw some great work from Poveda that ended with the ball across the box. Rodrigo waiting in the centre had his arm pulled back and went down so we should have been awarded a penalty. The referee played on as Leeds continued to put pressure on their defence. Poveda and Costa had made some great runs down the wings, but we could not capitalise on them. We were up against some giants again so needed to keep the ball on the floor. Crawley had a good run but were flagged offside.

My thoughts today were that we had to make sure we did not gift any goals to Crawley because a lot of the goals conceded this season have come from mistakes. This was highlighted when Poveda won the ball back from them, then a bad pass from Davis gave it back to them which I found frustrating. A great move involving Hernández; he passed the ball to Rodrigo who turned and shot. Although the final shot was not on target it was worth a go. A mistake from Phillips with a sloppy pass was pounced on by Crawley to run at Leeds and win a corner. Crawley sent a great corner over everyone to their man at the far post which brought a great save from Casilla from the header. That should have been a wake-up call for Leeds. Hernández tried once again to get his pass to Shackleton in the penalty area and it was a shame it did not come off. Costa and Poveda switched wings as we tried to change our attack with half-time looming but with no injury time played the whistle blew more or less on time. The commentators were saying they were surprised Leeds had not taken the game by the scruff of the neck. For me, it was a different team playing for us again so I felt we would grow into the game in the second half and did not anticipate any changes.

Well, what do I know? Bielsa obviously disagreed with me and brought on three subs at the start of the second half. With Harrison, Casey and Jenkins brought on for Rodrigo, Struijk and Cooper we changed our formation to a back four. I could see that due to Cooper coming back from injury that may have been an issue but would not have made the subs so early as it changed the game and weakened us as a team. That is not having a go at the players who came on, but Crawley had been strong in midfield in the first half anyway. Within six minutes of the restart, they had scored two goals in two minutes to go into the lead with the second one beating Casilla at the near post. I felt we had gifted them the game on a plate. It looked like we were not bothered about going forward in the cup and have thrown the towel in. I know my mood has not been great recently anyway and this contributed to me getting very angry about the whole game.

We did get behind the defence in a good move but with Costa being offside in the build-up I do not think it would have counted if it had gone in anyway. Sam Greenwood and Raphinha were then brought on for Davis and Poveda which provided a bit more to the team formation, but overall, we looked very ordinary and had no sense of urgency. To me Harrison playing in the middle had no effect and maybe we had too many playing out of position. Crawley were still the team looking more likely to score as Casilla put a shot around the post for a corner. There was a little and large situation with Shackleton man-marking but we managed to clear the ball. The game was over and done when Crawley scored a third goal from a free kick which saw Casilla save the first shot and they smacked the ball in from the rebound. They nearly got a fourth goal when they got through, but with Casilla right out of goal he did enough to put their player off and we got the ball away.

Crawley deserved their win, but I am cross with the decision to bring three subs on at the start of the second half which killed the game for me. We looked so unbalanced then and it gave Crawley the impetus. To me the FA Cup is still sacrosanct, and we should fight for it, but it seems we do not give a damn anymore which is unacceptable. For those fans who were not brought up with it like I was, which I find very sad, they only want to concentrate on the league. Having a good cup run as well as doing well in the league would be my ambition and give us fans something to savour in these challenging times. Sadly, it was not to be, again!

LUFC – Marching on Together!

LEEDS UNITED V BRIGHTON & HOVE ALBION; 16 JANUARY 2021 AT ELLAND ROAD

If anyone has not seen the thread I posted yesterday on social media, make sure you head over to the link on my website to be taken back to the terraces on the Kop in 1974. This is a blast from the past! An authentic cassette recording from Leeds United v Derby County on 6 April 1974, contains swearing. This was recorded by me, Heidi Haigh, a loyal Leeds United fan of over 50 years when I took my cassette recorder on to the Kop to record the singing of the fans. Enjoy listening to it and taking you back to a time when Leeds United were crowned First Division champions a few weeks later! To say the cassette has survived for nearly 47 years to keep those memories alive is brilliant plus it includes Ronnie Hilton's records at the end and thank you to him for giving us a chance to sing those songs on the terraces.

http://www.followmeandleedsunited.co.uk/a-blast-from-the-past-leeds-united-kop-v-derby-6th-april-1974-authentic-recording-done-by-heidi-haigh-contains-swearing

The rumours about Meslier not playing turned out to be true and with Phillips suspended for the game today it meant a reshuffle of the team.

Team: Casilla, Dallas, Ayling, Cooper, Alioski, Struijk, Raphinha, Rodrigo, Bamford, Harrison, Klich.
Subs: Roberts for Rodrigo (64), Hernández for Alioski (66), Poveda for Raphinha (74).
Subs not used: Caprile, Davis, Llorente, Jenkins, Roberts, Costa, Shackleton.
Leeds lost the game 1-0.
Attendance: Zero, behind closed doors.
Referee: Kevin Friend.

With all the recent snow and rain, the pitch looked heavy and was cutting up in places very quickly. The good news is the pitch is going to be replaced at the end of the season according to Kinnear's programme notes today.

Leeds had a good chance early on after a great cross from Harrison saw Rodrigo put off by their defender in front of goal and he could not stick the ball into the net. Brighton ran through us from a throw-in and their player went down in the penalty area under a challenge from Ayling, but the referee waved play on. Klich had a shot over the bar on 15 minutes. From the goal kick, somehow Brighton suddenly ran through us and when I expected their player to pass to the wing, they passed into the penalty area. The final cross to the far side of the goal saw their man in the middle all on his own to put the ball into the net on 16 minutes. Leeds had been ball watching rather than the man who snuck in behind Ayling.

Bamford was flagged offside which I disputed as he was behind their man and shouted to the linesman to get a grip. Brighton still looked dangerous and were running rings around us when the ball deflected off Ayling and hit the underside of the crossbar and away. It felt like a practice match from our perspective with extremely poor passing and at one time I felt like I could go to sleep.

To me it was the aftermath of our FA Cup loss to Crawley where instead of winning breeding winning, we looked down and out at times. Raphinha was robbed of the ball as White, now playing for Brighton, ran forward into our box but Ayling and Struijk between them, in the penalty area, got the ball away. Leeds tried to attack but the ball rebounded off the referee in a good position, but the new rules meant the game was stopped. I was expecting a dropped ball but the next thing I saw the Brighton keeper had the ball, so I am not sure what happened next. We continued to attack but our final balls were rubbish. I felt really frustrated by the way Leeds were playing when first from a corner Raphinha's cross was easily picked up by their keeper in the middle, then instead of going forwards, we passed back for the move to start again. Harrison, playing his 100th game for us, had played really well on the left-hand side but then switched sides with Raphinha very early in the game which didn't make sense to me. As it turned out Harrison is the only player today who did something. Any time we did manage to get forward the keeper easily gathered the crosses. It feels like our pitch is impeding our players for some reason at this moment, more than it does the opposition. Brighton still managed to do one-touch passing whilst ours seemed to have disappeared. I was feeling at a loss on how to change things as Raphinha kept trying long passes, but none were reaching our players. Ayling was booked when he caught the toes of their player, but I did not think it was too bad a foul. As it was coming up to half-time and their player stayed down, time-wasting came to mind. It was a relief when the whistle blew on what had been a rubbish half for Leeds United.

We certainly needed to up our game in the second half as we have been extremely poor. My thoughts were that we should make changes but at the time I did not know who, apart from changing our formation and try Rodrigo and Bamford up front.

There were no changes at the restart and after a few minutes into the second half, I felt totally demoralised. As Brighton attacked, we were standing watching them before letting them shoot wide. Leeds started attacking more as we changed formation with two up front and a good move ended with a final shot from Harrison that went wide across the goal. Some good work from Ayling saw him cross the ball to the left which was picked up by Raphinha. He did well to get past their defenders, but the final ball was too long and nowhere near any of our men. As we gave a silly ball away again it gave Brighton a chance, but luckily for us the shot went over the bar. Our passing was way too short as we kept giving the ball away and if that was not a wake-up call for Leeds, I don't know what is.

Roberts came on followed by Hernández as we tried to get back into the game as to me getting back on level terms would make a difference, but I could not see us scoring. Roberts had our first shot on target on 65 minutes that was saved by their keeper after a great pass from Bamford. At least we were looking more balanced now as we had a good ten-minute spell of attacking although we never got any clear chances on goal. Roberts won a free kick after having his shirt pulled but it came to nothing. Despite the game being so frustrating, getting a goal would be a relief. Our passing never improved though, and we always tried to make a final pass instead of trying to shoot.

We won a couple of corners in quick succession but with the latter one could not beat the first man. The Brighton team were dictating the play and suddenly had a shot with Casilla out of goal, but luckily he saved it even though he spilled the ball and caught it at the second attempt. Although we had a lot of possession it felt like we were trying to walk the ball into the net but with one attack, Brighton were awarded a free kick from a Bamford shot. Why, I had no idea. With Harrison being the only stand-out player for me today, I have not got anything positive to say about the game. The game once again had that déjà vu feeling about it and you could just tell that nothing was going to work for us today. A bad day at the office all round as well as a frustrating one. It is a good job we have a break now due to the Southampton game being postponed for an FA Cup game to take place. At least by sleeping on things, I can forget about this bad week for football as a Leeds fan.

LUFC – Marching on Together!

NEWCASTLE UNITED V LEEDS UNITED; 26 JANUARY 2021 AT ST JAMES' PARK

With the Southampton game postponed, the pitch at Elland Road will have been replaced by the time we play our next home game against Everton in February. I have seen the sum of £300,000 mentioned with the HT Pro hybrid pitch the same as at Tottenham and Swansea. This is a temporary replacement as the pitch is due for reconstruction at the end of the season along with a new drainage system. Also, Leeds announced further investment into the club by an affiliated entity of the 49ers with the increase of their share holding to 37 per cent. Paraag Marathe now becomes the vice-chairman of Leeds United.

Team: Meslier, Cooper, Llorente, Dallas, Harrison, Ayling, Raphinha, Rodrigo, Bamford, Phillips, Alioski.
Subs: Struijk for Llorente (10), Klich for Alioski (55), Roberts for Bamford (59).
Subs not used: Casilla, Poveda, Hernández, Costa, Davis, Shackleton.
Leeds won the game 2-1 with goals scored by Raphinha (17) and Harrison (61).
Attendance: Zero, behind closed doors.
Referee: Anthony Taylor.
Booked: Alioski, Harrison, Rodrigo.

My stomach had been churning for hours before the game today so I was a little nervous knowing how important a win would be. In the opening minutes of the game numerous players were injured and then Llorente went down and had to be replaced after ten minutes. Once again with a comeback game, Llorente has found himself injured. This was a big blow for us especially as he has spent more time on the treatment table than on the pitch since he

arrived at Leeds. It would have been nice to see him get a full game under his belt but sadly it was not to be. Hopefully, he was just taken off as a precaution.

A fantastic cross from Dallas to Harrison at the far post looked like it would be slammed into the net, but he did not connect with the ball right and the chance went wide. Leeds won a few corners in quick succession before taking the lead after some great build-up play, when Rodrigo pulled a great pass back across the penalty area for Raphinha on the edge of the box to score on 17 minutes. It was Meslier's turn to be treated by the trainer after he got a knee in the face and was down on the deck.

Leeds had the most possession and great moves in the first half but just before half-time, Newcastle went on a run and won a corner. Meslier dropped the cross but in front of Struijk who shielded the ball to him. Leeds had a couple of good chances prior to that with some great moves and Rodrigo was unlucky not to get on the scoresheet. Raphinha found himself knocked over by Ayling in their penalty area whilst we were on the attack. I was quite surprised to see the referee keep his yellow cards in his pocket as I felt there were a few tackles that warranted a booking, especially the one who caught the back of Raphinha's ankle. We nearly got complacent when Cooper glanced a short ball back to Meslier that put us under pressure, but Meslier was quickly out to smother the ball. Due to all the stoppages, it was no surprise to see five minutes of injury time added on. Leeds ended the half on the attack and some of the passes cutting through the Newcastle defence were sublime, but they battled to keep us out as the whistle blew just when we had won another corner.

At the start of the second half, Leeds were unlucky not to go further into the lead after a great ball from Raphinha saw the ball rebound off Dallas and into the net, but the goal was disallowed for handball. It was still a stop-start game due to injuries, but with Leeds a man down, the referee played on, and Newcastle won a corner. The resulting shot from them was straight at Meslier. Just after that Meslier took another knee to his face and needed treatment. The poor lad was certainly in the wars today. Bielsa brought Klich on to replace Alioski on 55 minutes and I thought we needed to change things to get back on top. With Newcastle coming out for the second half rejuvenated, sadly for us they scored straight away after the substitution. The goal came from a Leeds mistake when we had won the ball back but then gave it away too easily. Although Meslier got his hands to it, the pace of the ball and with our defence beaten, it meant he did not stand a chance of stopping the ball going into the net. Roberts came on to replace Bamford, but Leeds managed to get in front again a few minutes later. A glorious ball once again from Raphinha reached Harrison on the left-hand side and this time he made no mistake and slammed the ball into the net.

Leeds were having to battle when Struijk took the ball off their toes in our penalty area as Newcastle upped their game. Rodrigo sent a fantastic ball to Raphinha, and the final ball was just out of reach of Roberts. That had been a good chance. Newcastle won a couple

of corners as the final header went over the top of the bar. One challenge by Leeds, which I thought was a 50/50 tussle, saw their player fall over and awarded a free kick in a good position. Newcastle had certainly woken up this half especially when a fantastic save from Meslier denied them an equaliser. They then ran all the way through us with Roberts having no chance of catching their player, which brought another fantastic save from Meslier. There was no pressure on their player from us but also, we could not bring their player down either in a crucial position. Newcastle won another free kick outside the area and were looking strong down the left-hand side of the pitch towards our goal. Rodrigo was booked for diving; he had been tackled from behind and then their player retaliated putting his head in Rodrigo's face, so he got out of the way! Their player was bleeding in the mouth, but any contact was accidental. I thought Newcastle were the ones being antagonistic anyway. Ayling's cross was put out over the bar for a corner to Leeds then a deflection from Klich was put out for another one. Raphinha had a header come off their player and caught by their keeper as the whistle went for full time. Raphinha played well today and won a deserved man of the match

That was a hard-fought 2-1 win especially during the second half, so getting three points was vital. With the forthcoming Leicester game being on Sunday at least we have a few days for Llorente to recover.

LUFC – Marching on Together!

LEICESTER CITY V LEEDS UNITED; 31 JANUARY 2021 AT THE KING POWER STADIUM

After another night, this week where I was wide awake until gone 4am, I suppose I should be thankful I did not have to be in Leeds a few hours later to travel to the game. There again, I would much rather have been there with our fans as I can always sleep on the coach.

Team: Meslier, Cooper, Struijk, Ayling, Alioski, Phillips, Dallas, Rodrigo, Harrison, Bamford, Raphinha.
Subs: Klich for Rodrigo (21), Costa for Raphinha (80).
Subs not used: Casilla, Roberts, Shackleton, Poveda, Hernández, Davis, Cresswell.
Leeds won the game 3-1 with goals from Dallas (15), Bamford (71) and Harrison (84).
Attendance: Zero, behind closed doors.
Referee: Chris Kavanagh.
Booked: Ayling, Dallas.

Alioski was penalised for a foul which gave Leicester an early free kick to the right of the penalty area, but they went for a shot that went straight over the bar. Bamford was being tightly marked and given no room with at least three Leicester players crowding him out. I thought it was a nice touch from Leicester when it was announced they were wearing black armbands for laundry lady Sheila Kent, who had worked at their club for 40 years.

Leeds had a good move but the final ball to Bamford was just out of his reach. Sadly, Leicester took an early lead in the 13th minute. It was a simple move in the end after our ball across the pitch was too short. Leicester ran through the middle, and we were caught out as they were too fast, and the ball was put wide of Meslier to score. My heart sank at that moment.

As Ayling went on a run down the wing shortly afterwards and passed to Bamford, I shouted for us to get an instant reply. Well, I got my wish as within two minutes of them scoring Bamford gave a pinpoint pass to Dallas who hit a sweet strike past their keeper Schmeichel, an ex-Leeds player. What a goal and just what we needed! Dallas had scored in the home defeat by Leicester earlier in the season too.

Rodrigo went down injured after he stretched for a ball and eventually Leeds put the ball out for him to get treatment. I just thought no, please do not let anyone go off injured today, as it was very important we kept a settled side. My heart sank again when another goal went in for Leicester but I cheered up immediately when the flag went up for offside in what was an important decision for us. Sadly, Rodrigo went down injured again and did have to go off, going straight down the tunnel for further treatment. At least I was happy that Klich came on as his replacement. It was a shame a ball did not bounce high enough to go over their keeper's head and into the goal for us. Harrison was not strong enough to keep the ball on the wing but chased back immediately to prevent the ball going out for a corner.

A few minutes later a great cross over to Harrison saw him hit the ball first time without hesitation, which brought a good save out of their keeper to give Leeds a corner. As Klich put the ball into the net from close range after the keeper made a great save from a Bamford header, we saw the flag had gone up after Klich had strayed offside. Leeds kept up the pressure as the keeper had to make another great save from Raphinha to stop us taking the lead. Meslier was then called into action to boot the ball away as we looked open at the back and then smothered another shot shortly after. Leicester were forced to make a change just before the break due to their player having a groin injury. Ayling ended up in the book when he brought their man down with his arm as there was no way he was catching him. Is he suspended now? I was not sure for certain.

In the closing minutes of the half Leeds won a free kick when they were all over Bamford after loads had been given to them, but we were not able to keep the ball after they cleared our corner. I was desperate for them not to score before the whistle went for half-time as Leeds crowded them out in the penalty area. I breathed a sigh of relief after they nearly got through again, but Meslier saved the first shot and pounced on the ball at the second attempt just before injury time. Well done, Leeds, keep them out at all costs. It was nice to see their player not make a meal out of it after staying down when Alioski stood on top of his foot as the advantage was played. A good move from Leeds saw Harrison run out of pitch to cross the ball, which was a shame, as the last minutes of injury time seemed to drag but we went in at half-time on level terms.

Leicester made another change at the start of the second half as they started on the attack and put Leeds under pressure. We must watch our back line as Struijk made a great block for a corner but there was no one marking their two spare men in front of Meslier. Ayling needed treatment for bleeding on his forehead as play carried on whilst he was getting treated. I did not see what had happened though. Meslier made a couple of vital saves with some brave keeping. I thought Cooper was in danger of being sucked in to conceding free kicks when he was penalised for a foul; he had been lucky Leicester were not awarded a penalty when he pulled their player's shirt in the penalty area and brought him down. Luckily for us VAR and Mike Dean said no problem as play carried on.

Leicester were still on the attack as Dallas went to left-back to cover for Alioski, who ran forwards. Meslier had to make a couple more saves to keep them out before Dallas was booked for bringing their player down when beaten. Good play from Struijk in defence then he was seen flying through the air from a foul further up the pitch which won Leeds a free kick. After all the Leicester attacking suddenly, Leeds took charge of the game after winning the ball back, then three passes and the ball was in the net. A pinpoint pass from Raphinha saw Bamford hit a fantastic shot into the top right of the goal to put us into the lead with 14 minutes of normal time left. Absolutely brilliant, Leeds.

Leicester looked to make another change, but their player did not come straight on as they upped the pressure again with Leeds now leading. Klich's late challenge saw us get another yellow card. From the resulting free kick Phillips at the far post was caught out as their player got in behind him to cross the ball which we put out for a corner. It was a heart in our mouths time as the ball came across the box, as they had two unmarked players bearing down on the back post but were able to breathe a sigh of relief as the ball went wide. A great save from Meslier, plus he caught another at the second attempt, kept Leicester out as they did not stop the pressure. Some good defending from Raphinha saw us battling as a team to keep them out. Raphinha was injured which saw Costa coming on to replace him and Leicester made their third substitution at the same time.

Leeds won a corner and Leicester had to kick the ball off the line to keep us out. Another fantastic run from Bamford after a pinpoint pass from Klich saw him through and as their player nearly caught up with him in the penalty area, he passed the ball across to Harrison in a better position to stick the ball into the net to put Leeds 3-1 up with six minutes remaining. A classic Leeds goal, Struijk defending, then attack and in the goal at the other end in seconds. Loved it! Get in Leeds, that will hopefully see us win the game.

Bamford was injured in the final minutes, but he said afterwards that it was cramp so that is a relief. He was my man of the match which was also confirmed by Sky. That was a great win for us as Leicester had been unbeaten in seven games and were riding high amongst the top teams of the table. Although our position in the table had not changed, we have 29 points and are only four points off the top six places. Keep going Leeds, keep aiming for the top and having those fantastic goals to cheer today makes it all worthwhile.

LUFC – Marching on Together!

CHAPTER 6 – FEBRUARY 2021

LEEDS UNITED V EVERTON; 3 FEBRUARY 2021
AT ELLAND ROAD

After the heavy snow yesterday and rain since, we will see how our new pitch holds up. A minute's applause was held for 100-year-old Captain Tom after his death yesterday, who raised nearly £33m for the NHS. After Southampton were beaten 9-0 yesterday, Leeds went up to 11th place as that affected their goal difference which was inferior to ours. Rodrigo has been for a scan and hopefully his injury is not too bad thus giving Klich his chance to play today. Raphinha had recovered from his thigh injury to retain his place in the team.

Team: Meslier, Cooper, Ayling, Dallas, Alioski, Struijk, Bamford, Raphinha, Klich, Harrison, Phillips.
Subs: Roberts for Klich (69), Hernández for Alioski (78), Costa for Harrison (87).
Subs not used: Casilla, Davis, Shackleton, Huggins, Jenkins, Cresswell.
Leeds lost the game 2-1 with Raphinha scoring for Leeds (48).
Attendance: Zero, behind closed doors.
Referee: Michael Oliver.
Booked: Ayling, Harrison.

Leeds nearly caught Everton out after a quick throw-in got Leeds into the penalty area and won us an early corner. From the corner they cleared the ball to one of ours but instead of pushing straight back with an attack, the ball went back to Meslier, and the chance was lost. The new pitch looked to be holding up well in the early stages of the game, but we were slipping and sliding a lot. Everton were not so it must be down to the studs our players have on their boots.

Everton had a great run down the wing where they managed to get a good cross in after beating Raphinha. Struijk was at the near post, but the cross reached the man behind him all on his own with only Meslier to beat, to give Everton an early lead. You had better not be cheering, Mr Pope! A minute later Meslier had to make the save to prevent them getting another goal. Leeds immediately tried to hit back and a great shot from Klich was put out for a corner by the keeper. As Raphinha was stood waiting to take the corner he could not, as the linesman stood in front of him preventing him from taking it, as VAR was looking at something. Harrison was booked for a foul, but I did not think it warranted a booking. Leeds had another good move, but Bamford's header went over the bar. Some nice play from Bamford saw Leeds win another corner where a brilliant first-time strike from Alioski brought another save from the keeper. Leeds continued with some sustained pressure but then Everton tried getting back into the game and always looked dangerous. A great free kick from Phillips saw a Struijk header deflected by their player and saved by the keeper. Leeds continued to win lots of corners as they tried getting back into the game, but Everton were always a threat going forward and brought a further save from Meslier. They were also pulled up for offside in an attack, but I did not think it was.

There was some end-to-end football with each team closing each other down. The pitch was definitely slippy but it was not cutting up like it had been doing, which was good to see. Some nice play saw Bamford cutting out their pass, but he was quickly closed down. Everton were through again with a man spare, but they shot instead which went wide. Three minutes from the end of normal time in this half saw Everton increase their lead. They scored from a corner when they headed the ball on to their man at the back post who had lost his marker. Everton had another free kick in a dangerous place, but Leeds cleared the ball. Although we were losing by two goals, the game is not over yet as Leeds can still fight back.

At the start of the second half, they did exactly that as Leeds pulled a goal back within three minutes when Raphinha scored after good work from Harrison and Bamford. The ball seemed to run for Everton where they put in another dangerous cross although Leeds won the resulting thrown-in. Leeds were then very unlucky not to get an equaliser when we had two chances saved on the line, first from Klich, then Raphinha, before the keeper made another save from Harrison. Their keeper is having a blinder here. Leeds were forced to defend a free kick before Everton ran through us again but their final shot was wide. Leeds were not giving up and made our first sub with Roberts coming on for Klich. It was a very fast-paced game as Leeds still had to defend when Struijk battled with their player on the wing to put the ball out for a throw-in. Some more persistent play from Bamford saw the ball just over the crossbar.

It had been all Leeds this half, but Everton were always looking dangerous on the break which brought some vital defending from Cooper. Alioski looked like he could not keep on his feet, but the ball was maybe too far in front of him. He was then taken off with Hernández coming on to replace him with Dallas going to left-back. Ayling then found himself in the book. As their player was being subbed, he was time wasting, and the referee had to tell him to get off the pitch quicker. As he should have gone off the other side of the pitch, why was he allowed to dictate this? I had not given up yet as there is always time until the final whistle blows. Everton got through again through sheer persistence, but Meslier caught the cross easily. Leeds were not playing badly so there was still a chance as that never-say-die attitude meant we were still attacking. Harrison won a corner which I thought should have been a free kick to Leeds for a foul, then Roberts won a free kick in a similar place to the left of the goal.

As Everton cut out Hernández's pass there were three of their players through bearing down on our goal, but Meslier was quickly off his line and blocked their attempt as we

not quite as fluent as we have come to expect and the condition of the pitch looked quite poor. That should have been put right for tonight's game as a new hybrid pitch has been laid to improve the playing surface for the remainder of the season. A complete pitch reconstruction will take place at the end of the season. That should be great news for the players and help our passing style.

Enjoy the game.

Chris Hall

FULLERTON PARK

Here is Heidi Haigh's grandson Freddie Moss finally fitting into this season's kit. Freddie had a very challenging start to his life, being born nine weeks premature at the start of our promotion season. He loves hearing "Marching On Together" and "The Whites Are Going Up" being sung to him so he is born to be Leeds. Once a Leeds fan, always a Leeds fan!

Detectives pig). Diane was a lifelong Leeds United fan and valued branch member who passed away at the tender age of 26; her father Richard Cowan also a lifelong fan and is an original Darlington Branch member.

MG is a lifelong debilitating condition which affects every muscle in the body. Former Leeds legend Norman Hunter was a great supporter of this cause as his daughter Claire also suffers with this condition. Any contribution will go towards research into this little-known illness. If you wish to donate you can do online at www.myaware.org/appeal/donate – the Darlington Branch says "Thank you".

Anyone wanting to join or re-join or do a bit more to help run Darlington & District Branch can email Kim Rowling at kirowling@gmail.com or via the Darlington Leeds United Supporters Club Facebook page.

59

---

came away with the ball. That was always going to be a danger with us pushing up for an equaliser. I could not believe how quickly the game had gone past, but it had been very entertaining. Harrison was replaced by Costa as we tried a final push to get a goal back. When Everton pulled Raphinha back they were very lucky as they were so close to doing it in the penalty area. With five minutes' injury time on the clock, Leeds continued attacking and some great play saw Ayling's shot career off their player for a corner.

An excellent cross from Costa saw Everton clear the ball and although it felt like a goal for us was not going to happen, you never know. I think you could tell that Hernández had not been playing for a while as he just was not sharp enough at times, but it was good to see him getting some game time. As the whistle blew for full time it was hard lines Leeds as they had played well and never given up. With our next game not until Monday against Crystal Palace, we have a bit of a breather now.

Having just received my Leeds United mishmash from Alex Bennett (@footymishmash on Twitter), I am proud to say I made the final publication. It is good to see although I have no idea where I am going to put it!

LUFC – Marching on Together!

LEEDS UNITED V CRYSTAL PALACE; 8 FEBRUARY 2021 AT ELLAND ROAD

With another lot of recent snow and heavy rain our new pitch will be put to the test again.

Team: Meslier, Cooper, Phillips (making his 200th appearance), Ayling, Alioski, Struijk, Harrison, Dallas, Raphinha, Klich, Bamford.
Subs: Shackleton for Phillips (88).

Subs not used: Casilla, Gelhardt, Shackleton, Cresswell, Davis, Jenkins, Costa, Huggins.
Leeds won the game 2-0 with goals from Harrison (3) and Bamford (52).
Attendance: Zero, behind closed doors.
Referee: Andre Marriner.

Leeds got off to a great start with a goal after three minutes when a brilliant deflection from Harrison's shot went over the keeper's head and into the net. Looking at the colour of some of the players' boots today, I cannot say I have noticed many wearing black boots before as they are normally an array of different colours. It could be they had changed boots to wear the correct studs for the pitch, but there were still a few players slipping on the surface, Klich and Ayling – who looked to get hurt – plus some Palace players. Another good move saw a Bamford header saved at the foot of the post by their keeper. Palace won a corner which was cleared by Leeds then some good movement from Bamford saw him head a cross wide, then another chance saw his shot go over the crossbar. A foul on Raphinha just outside the box in a good position saw his free kick go over the top of the goal.

Leeds were taking their time moving forwards with a lot of passing across our back four and not going forward. Maybe we were taking a more cautious approach in defence today but at times I wanted to move the ball forward. Playing too deep was inviting Palace to attack but maybe that is what Bielsa wanted from us, but it was quite frustrating at times. I thought we may give Palace too much hope, especially when Meslier had to be on alert to make a save. Cahill was lucky not to concede a penalty when he dragged Raphinha down and he went down in the box, but the tackle was outside the area. A couple of good moves saw Struijk making his presence known in the box but with one, the final shot went over the bar and another his header went wide. We were getting chances, but we needed them to count. A Raphinha free kick saw Cooper get a header in which was easily caught by their keeper, but he did well to get into a position to challenge the ball.

When Struijk headed the ball under a challenge in their penalty area, the commentator called him a 50p head. I am assuming it is something to do with swivelling on the ball but I am sure someone will enlighten me. Just before the break it looked like Palace were through our defence as their player went down looking for a penalty, but play was waved on. That could have been very costly. At least we had been in good positions during the first half; all we need is for them to count.

Things got off to a slightly slower start in the second half but enough for Leeds to take a two-goal lead on 52 minutes. A great shot from Raphinha was saved by their keeper but Bamford following up put the rebound into the net to give us that cushion with his 12th goal of the season. Palace started running at us more as they tried to get back into the

Photo courtesy Yorkshire Evening Post – Kop Committee Peter Lorimer Testimonial.

game with their final shot over the bar from a good position, then Meslier saved another shot. A good Leeds move going forward saw Bamford in a great position waiting for the ball, but the cross went behind him. That was a shame as it deserved more. Phillips was hurt and required treatment. Raphinha was having a fantastic game and involved in a lot of moves as well as seeing their keeper make a save at the near post for a corner. Justice was served after a dirty foul on Dallas got them a booking. A fantastic shot from Harrison hit the crossbar and careered off the top at speed, what a shame.

Ayling looked as if he was going on a run forward only to stop and pass the ball back which looked like we were making sure we did not leave our defence wide open. When Phillips went down injured again that was to be his last part in the game as Shackleton came on to replace him with three minutes of normal time left. It is not often we get to that part of the game with no subs made. Not a good end for Phillips with this being his 200th game for the club as Dallas stepped into his role. Meslier was called upon to make a save as the game neared injury time, but I did not want Palace to have a lifeline with a goal, or hope, in the final minutes of the game. Leeds continued to keep possession passing the ball back and across the back line as our cautious approach suddenly opened up for us to attack. Sadly, although it put Palace under pressure no one was close enough to knock the final ball in.

Raphinha won a deserved man of the match and once again he was mine too. The game may not have been a classic, but a win is a win and another three points saw Leeds go up to tenth in the table. After 9,000 Leeds fans last saw Leeds at the Emirates Stadium, it would have been so nice to head there next Sunday this time for a Premier League clash. Sadly, we are still playing behind closed doors so will have to make do with watching it on TV.

LUFC – Marching on Together!

ARSENAL V LEEDS UNITED; 14 FEBRUARY 2021 AT THE EMIRATES STADIUM

It does not seem two minutes since I was travelling by train to London after work to the FA Cup game. Timing was key to getting there at all, but everything worked liked clockwork before getting back at 3am and going into work four hours later. The things you do to support your team.

I thought I had definitely lost my marbles this week. Even though I was convinced that Leeds were playing today, Sunday, I checked the official website and the fixture was down for Saturday. I was geared up for that only to find out I was right in the first place when I started reading what other fans were posting. Having taken a screen print, I am pleased to report I did not imagine it which is a relief! It looks like the list in the fixtures part of the website never got updated with the changes.

I have just received my *United Revolución* book from Justin Slee which has some great photos in it and I am looking forward to reading more later. Thank you to Gerry Johnston for allowing me to appear on his show after the game today and I am looking forward to chatting to him again in future.

Team: Meslier, Cooper, Ayling, Dallas, Struijk, Alioski, Bamford, Raphinha, Harrison, Klich, Shackleton.
Subs: Costa for Harrison (45), Roberts for Klich (45), Huggins for Alioski (53).
Subs not used: Casilla, Cresswell, Davis, Hernández, Gelhardt, Jenkins.
Leeds lost the game 4-2 with Struijk (58) and Costa (68) getting the Leeds goals after being 4-0 down.
Attendance: Zero, behind closed doors.
Referee: Stuart Attwell.
Booked: Struijk, Dallas.

My heart sank when I saw that Struijk had been moved out of his strongest position in defence into Kalvin's role, with Shackleton brought in at right-back and Ayling moving to centre of defence. To me we would not play to our strengths with our players being out of position and should not have changed the back four when we knew it was working. I may not agree with the decision but as I always say, Bielsa has to do it his way.

Arsenal were immediately on the attack but their first couple of chances were way over the bar, but it was a sign of things to come. Although a good cross from Harrison brought a header from Bamford which was saved by their keeper, the game turned on its head two minutes later. A ball out of defence was picked up by Arsenal and they ran at us down the left-hand side and Meslier was beaten at the near post to given them an early 13th-minute lead. They managed to shoot between Ayling and Cooper when it looked like they were going to shoot in the opposite corner. That London hoodoo strikes again.

A good piece of play from Leeds ended with Klich's shot way over the bar as Leeds stepped up a gear. A great pass from Raphinha to Harrison saw their keeper gladly catch the ball. It was obvious that our formation was not working when Arsenal more or less walked through us, and we had to be thankful that Ayling's deflection put the ball over the bar for a corner. With the half-hour mark upon us we needed to change what we were doing. Arsenal were forcing us back and Meslier came close to seeing the ball whipped off his feet as he cleared it. I was not thinking of any subs coming on only changing our formation, but it felt like Bielsa wanted to get to half-time before making any changes to the team but that was to be our downfall.

With that Arsenal were awarded a penalty on 33 minutes after a Cooper challenge. I thought that their player went down easily as my other half thought it was definite penalty. As it was, VAR overruled the decision and we had been given a lifeline as Leeds went on to win a corner. Sadly, we could not beat the first man as they cleared it. With only 28 per cent possession for Leeds this half we had been up against it, but things got worse when we were forced back even though I screamed for us to pass the ball forward. Meslier stumbled when the ball was nearly whipped off his toes and with his second try for the ball, he caught their man too. This gave Arsenal a two-goal lead as this penalty sent Meslier the wrong way with 40 minutes on the clock.

In reality, we had been chasing shadows this half as Arsenal continued to make it look easy. They were queuing to put the ball into the net as Meslier was beaten at his near post and Leeds were 3-0 down on the stroke of half-time. It had certainly been a bad day at the office so to speak but I was adamant we should have changed our formation earlier. Let us see what the second half brings, it will either be a fightback from us or annihilation. At this moment, I could not see us getting anything out of this game but was happy to be proved wrong.

As I thought Hernández may come on for Alioski, I was wrong. Instead, Costa and Roberts replaced Harrison and Klich. The second half saw us get off to a disastrous start as Costa was not strong enough to keep the ball and the next thing the ball was in the net

Photo courtesy Yorkshire Evening Post – Kop Committee.

and Leeds 4-0 down. Well, we certainly do things in style. Leeds were not totally down and out though as they brought some pride back to the team with some fight still in there. A great shot from Raphinha brought a save out of their keeper before another attack won Leeds a corner. A powerful header from Struijk from this corner pulled one back for us. Arsenal were nearly through again attacking our goal with Raphinha chasing back from the halfway line, but our defence broke it up. That is the good thing about this team, they never give up fighting. I've no idea what happened to Costa as his mouth was bleeding, but it maybe fired him up as he scored Leeds a second goal after a good run and cross from Roberts down the wing.

Struijk was booked but even when watching the replay, I could not see why. Someone will enlighten me in time no doubt, but Arsenal had lots of space on the wing since Alioski went off. Bamford was unlucky when he made a great run down the centre of the pitch and was crowded out in the penalty area. He deserved a goal for that run. The woodwork saved Leeds from another Arsenal goal from the counter-attack, and they still looked dangerous going forward. Arsenal looked like they were going to score another goal, but the ball hit the post and rebounded as Leeds won a free kick for a foul on Raphinha. I was surprised their man did not get a booking as it was after the ball had gone. Even though we were losing I was still willing the ball into the net as we ended the half still fighting. Arsenal came the closest to scoring though, bringing out a good save from Meslier and were breaking away when Dallas fouled their man and ended up with a booking.

We did not disgrace ourselves in the second half, but the game was already lost by half-time realistically. We will not win every game, that is for sure, but need to fight back with the game at Wolves on Friday. As this game is also still showing as a Saturday fixture on the official website, I will ensure I do not take any notice of that one!

LUFC – Marching on Together!

WOLVERHAMPTON WANDERERS V LEEDS UNITED; 19 FEBRUARY 2021
AT MOLINEUX

With Alioski on the bench and Roberts coming into the team, it looked like a slight change of formation today. With Dallas going to left-back, Struijk back in defence in his strongest position, Ayling back at right-back this pushed Shackleton into Phillips's role. Although recently injured, Phillips lost his gran this week too.

Team: Meslier, Cooper, Ayling, Bamford, Roberts, Raphinha, Dallas, Struijk, Harrison, Klich, Shackleton.
Subs: Hernández for Shackleton (66), Alioski for Klich (81), Costa for Harrison (81).
Subs not used: Casilla, Llorente, Davis, Gelhardt, Jenkins, Huggins.
Leeds lost the game 1-0.
Attendance: Zero, behind closed doors.
Referee: David Coote.

A good run out of defence saw a Roberts pass to Bamford win Leeds a corner that was cleared by Wolves. When all I could think about was the Netto supermarket (long gone) after hearing the name, I knew the Wolves player would be a pain in the arse against us today. Another attack by Leeds saw Roberts let the ball run instead of having a go himself, but the chance was lost as no other Leeds player was close enough to pick the ball up. Wolves were very quick once they broke up our attack as they raced out of defence but luckily Dallas put the ball out for a corner. Wolves had their long-range shooting boots on today with the first one saved by Meslier. He was called into action again to save another shot after Wolves made it hard for us to play out from the back, putting us under pressure.

With Lucy Ward, ex-Leeds, commenting on the game, my heart sank when she said that Wolves had not opened the scoring in 14 games which was later repeated by her colleague. Despite being told that my superstitions do not decide games, the comments came back to haunt us as it was odds on that would happen! A shot from Raphinha bounced easily for their keeper to gather the ball. As I was thinking Roberts needs to be tough tonight, he was pulled up for a foul but even though their player went down hurt, it did not look that

103

bad a challenge. Roberts was involved in some good movements going forward in the opening minutes of the half. Wolves then had another long-range shot that brought a save out of Meslier.

A foul from behind on Bamford saw Leeds awarded a free kick. A great delivery from Raphinha picked Cooper out and his glancing header was straight at the keeper. As Wolves came forward again, their man was all alone on the wing with Ayling coming back from an attacking position. We need to watch that we do not give them too much space. With their player leaning into Struijk he eventually won a free kick when he ended up on the floor although I did not think it was a foul. There was no way he was going to stay on his feet. Leeds came so close to opening the scoring just before the half-hour mark when the bottom of the post saved them from Klich's shot and a second shot from Struijk was saved by the keeper. As Wolves raced out of defence, Meslier was forced into making another great save to keep them out. I was more than happy with our formation today despite Wolves having plenty of attacks.

When the commentator mentioned Robin Cook, I thought who is he before realising he meant Koch. Wolves were proving they were not a pushover when they got through our defence again as Meslier covered his near post and put the ball out for a corner. Raphinha put some great crosses into the box only for them to be just out of reach of our incoming players. If only we had got longer legs! Meslier was alert and had to be quick out of his area to kick the ball away. A great throw from Meslier to Raphinha put Leeds on the attack but it did not come to anything. Some good defending saw Cooper win the ball, but as Wolves picked the ball up first, he was shouting at Roberts to track back. Leeds tried going forward again and were unlucky it did not come off after some good work from Harrison. It had been a very quick half as the whistle blew just after 45 minutes had been played without any injury time added on. It is rare to see that as normally at least a minute is added on. With the score evenly balanced at 0-0 it was anyone's game.

The start of the second half saw Wolves closing us down well, making Leeds work around them patiently to start an attack. They continued to keep forcing us back which is something I do not want to do if I can help it, although it cannot be avoided at times. At one point Ayling's run with the ball took him right over to the opposite side of the field. Harrison was bundled off the ball, but Cooper won it back only for Wolves to come at us again, but their shot was over the top of our goal. Struijk made a couple of great passes across the field and Raphinha was also displaying his skills with a great ball to Bamford. Ayling then followed suit with a great pass that won a corner. Klich won a free kick when hit on the back of the head and their keeper made a point-blank save from Cooper to prevent Leeds taking the lead with Bamford's follow-up shot cleared off the line. How cruel then to see Wolves run to the other end and hit a long-range shot that bounced off the corner of the crossbar and hit Meslier on his back and into the net. The jammy sods and it shows what a bit of luck can do; I was gutted for Meslier.

Hernández came on for Shackleton as Leeds were awarded a free kick. A fantastic cross from Raphinha, which Cooper got to, saw their keeper very lucky to put the ball out for a corner. After having so many years where we have been dire at free kicks, crosses into the box and corners, it was nice to see that they were causing problems for Wolves now with Raphinha taking them. As we are getting stronger in that respect, the goals will come in time. When a perfect through ball to Bamford saw him run forwards and smash an unstoppable shot into the net, it was disallowed for offside. Even though the VAR line showed him level, he must have been offside by a fingernail! That hit home hard and yes it may show differently from another angle, but having the attacker given the advantage as used to be in the rules is sorely missed. Wolves were certainly riding their luck today to still be in the lead. Our goal being disallowed made me so angry as that would have been game on and a chance for us to win the game.

Costa and Alioski came on for Klich and Harrison before Wolves subbed their earlier substitute for an injury. A good through ball from Raphinha was just too long for Roberts to reach, the latter then winning us a corner after a great ball from Hernández. A shot from Roberts hit their player on the head and he went down in the penalty area which stopped our attack. With that Wolves were given the advantage as new rules meant they were given the ball when we had been in possession of it. That to me is all wrong.

Good defending from Struijk meant Wolves won a corner but as they were time wasting taking it, their man was booked. With five minutes of injury time to play Wolves were keeping us in the corner at our end of the field. In the closing minutes Wolves had all the luck again when Roberts received a great pass from Raphinha, and the keeper saved the shot with his feet. If only he could have lifted the ball over the keeper. With our final chance in the game the keeper saved a header from Raphinha meaning Wolves won the game with that earlier lucky goal. If the original shot had gone in, that would have been easier to bear as it would have been a great goal. To get the luck they did for the shot to rebound off Meslier's back meant Leeds were unlucky to get defeated. We played well and deserved a draw which would have been a just result.

With our game against Aston Villa next Saturday having a 5.30pm kick off, I am hoping we can get back to winning ways.

LUFC – Marching on Together!

LEEDS UNITED V SOUTHAMPTON; 23 FEBRUARY 2021 AT ELLAND ROAD

With it being Trevor Cherry's birthday today I shared a couple of photos taken at the Amsterdam Tournament in 1976 with a banner made by my friend Carole as a tribute to him. Power to yer boot, Trevor! I am not sure if the wind had picked up in Leeds but if it is anything like in Halifax, it will make challenging conditions today. Leeds had 11 virtual mascots from Beeston Primary School.

Team: Meslier, Cooper, Ayling, Struijk, Llorente, Harrison, Klich, Raphinha, Bamford, Dallas, Roberts.
Subs: Costa for Harrison (45), Alioski for Klich (59), Hernández for Roberts (74).
Subs not used: Casilla, Gelhardt, Cresswell, Jenkins, Casey, Huggins.
Leeds won the game 3-0 with goals from Bamford (47), Dallas (78) and Raphinha (84).
Attendance: Zero, behind closed doors.
Referee: Andre Marriner.
Booked: Raphinha.

When Dallas stumbled in the first minute and then Llorente slipped, it was not looking good for playing on the new pitch as it looked wet. I am not sure if it had been watered before the game or not, but on seeing us unable to keep our footing, it would be an own goal in my opinion. Bielsa made a change to the formation with Struijk on the left-hand side of our defence and Llorente on the right. It looked like we did not have anyone specific in Phillips's role today with Harrison starting on the right wing and Raphinha on the left. With a good early chance, Bamford passed the ball for Roberts in the penalty area, but he was unable to reach it. Southampton looked dangerous when they got a free kick and although their player got to the ball from the cross and headed wide, hopefully Struijk did enough to put him off despite being blocked in the build-up. Meslier made a crucial save after they sent Cooper the wrong way and got a shot in. We made a few bad passes, but I was sure we would settle down.

Raphinha's free kick saw four of our players getting past the defence in the penalty area, but the flag was up for offside. It was a correct decision but also good to see them all trying to score. It was hard to know who was playing where at this moment. Llorente showed his class with a great ball to the opposite side of the pitch. The longer the game went on, the more concerned I was about the state of the pitch. For the money spent on it, have we been sold a dud? It was very slippy for both teams and looked to be cutting up in places. Although the weather may have impacted on the pitch settling in, that was not a good sign for me.

We saw some good defending from Ayling before Bamford was unlucky, getting pushed off the ball at the last minute in their penalty area. The commentators were doing my head in and is why I want to be there at the games, so I do not have to listen to them! We did keep giving the ball away a lot which worked in favour of Southampton, before we changed formation with Raphinha back on the right wing and Harrison back on the left. Leeds should have taken the lead shortly afterwards after fantastic work from Raphinha saw him pass a great ball to Roberts in the middle of the pitch, only to see him blast it over the top. That was a bad miss and in reality, he should have at least got it on target. Roberts was on the receiving end when he was brought down, which earned their player a booking for the foul. Even though we were a bit too far out to score, Raphinha sent a great ball to Llorente on the right with Dallas on the receiving end of his pass, who brought a save out of the keeper.

Meslier made a great save, but the referee gave Leeds a free kick for handball. The next minute Southampton were awarded a penalty after Llorente caught their man. When replays showed that he had not fouled their man, Kevin Friend in charge of VAR asked the referee to look at it again. On seeing the replays, the referee changed his mind which was the right decision. A brilliant ball out of defence from Dallas to Raphinha looked as if he was set to score but the ball was whipped off his toes in the penalty area. My first instincts were that it was a cast-iron penalty and sending off, but it just shows what happens when you see it again, as it proved to be an excellent tackle. Llorente gave the ball away but then struggled to get going again on the pitch which was a concern but luckily all was okay, and we cleared it. The ball had to be changed just before the break so hopefully that will benefit us. Cooper tried to shield the ball out, but Southampton got it but then he recovered to win it back. Southampton got the ball into the net, but as they had taken the free kick before the referee had blown his whistle, it was disallowed, and play brought back. Southampton came the closest to scoring from a corner which brought a save from Meslier as the ball swung in dangerously. With the score 0-0 at half-time, it had been quite an eventful half.

Costa replaced Harrison for the start of the second half which turned on its head very quickly. This meant Raphinha was back on the left wing again. After a good block from Struijk and a save from Meslier, Leeds took an early lead. A great pass from Roberts to Bamford saw him run forward, hit a low shot from just outside the area and into the net for a great start. Southampton tried getting straight back into the game which brought another save from Meslier. Leeds should have got a second goal after another amazing run from Raphinha, but the final shot was inches wide from Roberts. So close and a shame he did not bury it. We nearly scored again after a great clearance from Ayling saw Raphinha run to the other end, pass the ball to Dallas before Bamford saw his shot then the follow-up from Roberts, both saved by the keeper. Costa won a corner and once cleared with Southampton on the attack, he raced back to win the ball back and was brought down in the process. Some good defending from Cooper ended with Klich down in our penalty area so we put the ball out. Southampton made a double sub as Alioski came on to replace Klich. With that, Alioski went to left-back and Dallas moved into midfield.

Alioski nearly went flying when he tried stopping himself running forward. Some great play from Leeds after a pass from Alioski to Raphinha then Llorente brought a save by their keeper Alex McCarthy. To say he was on loan at Leeds one time, I cannot even remember him being here. Some fantastic defending on the line from Bamford made sure the ball was kept out even though Meslier was behind him. Better to be safe than sorry. A free kick awarded against Alioski was wrong as he did not touch him, their man was already falling down when Alioski kicked the ball away. The pitch was looking quite dangerous with the number of times players were slipping on the surface with Dallas one of them. As their player started walking off the pitch injured, he then went down to waste time for their sub to come on. Meslier saved another long-range shot but then as we got it away, they won it back and shot over the top, but it was offside anyway. Hernández replaced Roberts with just over 15 minutes of the game left.

Costa made a run down the wing and sent a great pass to Dallas who hit his shot through three men and past the keeper into the goal to give us a two-goal lead with little over ten minutes of the game left. Praise should go to Raphinha for his great run across the goal which created space for Dallas to get his shot in. Dallas held up a shirt after he scored with the name of Granny Val on, in memory of Phillips's grandma who died last week. Southampton were still putting us under pressure when they could and got through, although their player did not know much about it when his shot forced a save from Meslier. A Leeds counter-attack ended with Costa fouled but the free kick awarded was in a good position. A brilliant free kick from Raphinha straight into the bottom left of the goal with the keeper beaten saw us take a three-goal lead. As Raphinha took his shirt off to show some writing on his shirt it earned him a booking. I do not see anything wrong with taking your shirt off to celebrate anyway. Raphinha, who was to be crowned man of the match again, ran to close their keeper down which is the Bielsa way despite only a few minutes remaining. That is just what I want to see, Leeds battling until the final whistle blows.

Our formation was changed today and ignored the normal Phillips role so well done Bielsa as it proves he listens. Even though it took a while to get on top and there were some hairy moments, it worked. The last minutes saw Raphinha keeping the ball in play with his great pass to Alioski with the final shot from Hernández over the bar. An excellent three points sees Leeds climb to tenth in the table setting us up nicely for Saturday's game against Aston Villa.

LUFC – Marching on Together!

LEEDS UNITED V ASTON VILLA; 27 FEBRUARY 2021
AT ELLAND ROAD

The very sad news coming out on Thursday evening was hearing that Peter Lorimer is in a hospice battling his long-term illness and Mick Bates is also ill too. Having been brought up watching the greatest team on earth with the great Don Revie side, these players gave me the best part of my life travelling all over the world watching them play. Knowing that we could shortly be losing some more members of that team after Norman Hunter, Jack Charlton and Trevor Cherry's deaths last year moved me to tears. I know I was not the only one of our fans from that era feeling this way. My thoughts are with their families and friends at this moment and know there are thousands of us fans willing them both on.

Having been part of Peter Lorimer's testimonial committee where we helped to raise funds for it, those memories will always be there, and I cherish every moment. Make the most of life as we never know what is around the corner. The photos are from Peter Lorimer's testimonial committee and from the Don Revie statue fundraiser at the Plantation with the SLI with Mick Bates and Eddie Gray. I will always remember Mick telling me to definitely get my first book *Follow Me and Leeds United* published when speaking to him about it and I'm so glad I did. Everything in the book is true, but it also takes me back to a time where I followed Leeds United everywhere not missing a match home or away for seven years and went abroad to see them too. Despite being a girl in a man's world I would not change being there at all even though there were some horrible and torrid times too along with the violence, that meant you took your life in your hands just to follow your team. Character-building, I would call it today!

Team: Meslier, Cooper, Llorente, Struijk, Dallas, Ayling, Bamford, Raphinha, Klich, Costa, Roberts.
Subs: Alioski for Struijk (52), Harrison for Costa (64), Hernández for Roberts (71).
Subs not used: Casilla, Davis, Gelhardt, Cresswell, Huggins, Jenkins.
Leeds lost 1-0.
Attendance: Zero, behind closed doors.
Referee: Peter Bankes.
Booked: Klich, Roberts.

In the first minutes Bamford was through and his shot/pass beat Raphinha with the bounce of the ball as he came in at the far post. Villa were straight back on the attack and within five minutes were in the lead. When their man passed the ball to the right of the goal, it by passed all our players to reach their player seemingly in lots of space with Costa breathing

Don Revie Statue – South Leeds Independent – Eddie Gray, Heidi and Mick Bates.

down his neck, who hit the ball into the net. That was a blow, and I do not think we recovered after that. Although Struijk was playing in Phillips's role today, I thought it was a shame he was out of our defence having kept clean sheets whilst in that position. He did not do anything wrong today but as it is not his strongest position, I do not think we play better as a team with that formation.

Leeds had a chance when Raphinha's shot was blocked in the penalty area which rebounded to Roberts who saw his shot saved by their keeper. As we came forward Struijk pointed for Dallas to send the ball to the left but instead, he sent the ball to the right and sadly that was cut out by Villa as they came forward again winning another corner. They were putting us under pressure at corners that is for sure. Some good defending by Struijk in the corner won us a throw-in.

The commentators had to mention that Villa game [in 2019] where Bielsa let them score. That is one time I will never agree with the decision made by Bielsa as you play to the whistle. I still get angry that their players manhandled Klich and despite the number of replays shown, were never punished for bringing the game into disrepute. When I think of the injustices Leeds as a club have had with TV decisions going against them that were made after games had finished, for instance Bowyer and Beckford, it made a mockery of things for me.

Meslier saved a long-range shot at the second attempt but there was no danger of anyone being near enough to put the ball into the net for them. Dallas's shot was just wide after good play from Klich before the commentators said a foul on Dallas was only slightly late and a mistake! Noticing that Raphinha has his shorts tucked in made me wonder if that was why he ran so fast when he made a great run. Cooper's header from a corner was easily saved by their keeper. Costa got past their player then was pulled up for a foul, but replays showed minimal contact as he threw himself to the ground. It was noticeable that Villa players went down very easily at times. Another long-range shot by Villa was wide, but it looked like Meslier had it covered anyway.

Our best chance of the half so far came after a great ball from Struijk to Roberts saw him blast the ball over the top of the bar when at least he should have had it on target. Raphinha's movement on and off the ball is good to see. When their player went down holding his leg, Roberts pulled him up and of course he was fine. Leeds won a corner after good work from Raphinha who then sent the ball out to Costa on the edge of box to hit the ball low that won us another corner. From this one Roberts was too lax in the middle of the field and Villa won possession then ran all the way to the other end and saw their shot saved by Meslier. Leeds tried again from a free kick and a header from Ayling was easily caught by their keeper. Llorente was fouled and went down injured rolling about but was hauled up by their player. He was not limping then, and my thoughts were not to copy Villa as that is not the Leeds way. As we went in at half-time losing to that early goal, I would have made changes to the team for the start of the second half, bringing on Harrison and Hernández for Costa and Roberts. In my opinion they are not strong enough for 90 minutes and I would use them in a sub role only.

Bielsa kept the same side and although we were having flashes of brilliance, we were not setting the game alight. Alioski came on for Struijk but even after he came on no one was taking control of the game for us, which was crying out for Hernández, as it felt a bit like headless chickens at times. When Roberts was booked after being hauled down it looked like he had retaliated but their player was cheating again as there was no contact. Klich was booked just after that and I thought we were losing our cool and panicked; we should take both Klich and Roberts off now, so they did not get sent off. As the game continued, I calmed down and thought about my earlier days of following Leeds and getting booked did not automatically mean you would get sent off!

Harrison replaced Costa and shortly afterwards when Villa got a goal kick, their keeper was seen taking a tablet in the middle of the game. I felt that we were going to get nothing out of the game today as we were not gelling like we have done recently. Maybe the way the team was set up at the start today was wrong. Villa won the ball back and ran to other end but shot over as their other man was in acres of space at the other side of the goal. Hernández replaced Roberts with about 15 minutes of the game left. When the commentators were trying to blame Klich for blood on the Villa player's face, replays showed he was nowhere near him when he fell. They then decided the blood was already there! Leeds won a corner but the final ball from Klich went well over the bar. My hopes for getting anything out of the game were dwindling as Mings was taking the goal kick rather than the keeper. It was ages before the ball was kicked and I could not understand why it had taken so long apart from them time wasting of course. What was the referee doing?

We really needed an equaliser but all our attempts on goal were straight to the keeper. I have got to believe we could get something from the game but deep down I knew we would not. Good challenging from Harrison won Leeds a throw-in then Dallas was fouled from behind, but the free kick was given to Villa. Did I miss something? Was it handball or offside? Bamford was back defending as Villa's time-wasting continued. With challenges from them going amiss and Targett being a big culprit, the referee started being whistle happy in Villa's favour. When Hernández was booked after being fouled, I thought the referee was losing the plot, even if my lip reading told me Hernández told him to f**k off. Leeds then had our best chance of this half to equalise after Harrison came forward with the ball with Alioski free on his left, only to see his great cross find Raphinha on the right but his header went wide.

With five minutes' time added on the commentators surpassed themselves when saying Villa were now using time management to see the game out. Obviously, they did not have their eyes open as Villa had been doing it since their keeper did not take the goal kick. I do not think we played well today and maybe our starting line-up did not help, although maybe Villa not letting us play was more to do with that. With Leeds awarded a corner, the referee spoke to Targett again who was pushing Bamford about. When he did let the corner be taken, we should have been awarded a penalty when Targett brought Bamford down. Really, he should have already been off the pitch the number of times he was let off for fouls, but the referee was not strong enough to make that decision.

As the final whistle blew, knowing we had lost meant it was not to be. Although disappointing, we have to put this game behind us and focus on the next one, the visit to West Ham. This was one ground I was looking forward to visit as I had never been there just Upton Park their previous ground. Oh well, there is nothing I can do about that, but there's always next season!

LUFC – Marching on Together!

CHAPTER 7 – MARCH 2021

WEST HAM UNITED V LEEDS UNITED; 8 MARCH 2021
AT THE LONDON STADIUM

What I would have given to visit another new stadium tonight following Leeds United. At least things are getting closer to us fans being allowed back at grounds in some capacity. To say the powers that be are now looking at the integrity of the Premier League when they were not bothered before Christmas when some clubs had the luxury of some fans in attendance, makes me laugh. They did not bother about that, then, did they? We will see what happens next.

After reading the latest newsletter from LUST, the Leeds United Supporters' Trust, it was good to read that the away season tickets showing the loyalty of our support will be honoured. Getting back to home and away games will be relished and cannot come soon enough for me.

Team: Meslier, Cooper, Dallas, Ayling, Llorente, Phillips, Klich, Costa, Raphinha, Roberts, Bamford.
Subs: Alioski for Klich (45), Harrison for Costa (45), Rodrigo for Roberts (60).
Subs not used: Caprile, Poveda, Davis, Berardi, Jenkins, Huggins.
Leeds lost the game 2-0.
Attendance: Zero, behind closed doors.
Referee: Mike Dean.
Booked: Phillips.

Leeds started the game well and a great ball from Phillips to Costa saw him running down the wing and win us a corner. As West Ham cleared the ball it came back out to the left, but Roberts could not get the better of their defender to get a cross in. A powerful shot from Costa went over the crossbar. As Roberts hammered the ball into the net for Leeds, I thought we had scored a perfectly legitimate early goal only to see the flag go up for offside which was confirmed by VAR. I thought the offside rules were from when the ball was kicked not when the ball was received but with rules forever changing, I wasn't sure if that was still the case? Even seeing VAR did not convince me that the goal was offside although my hubby thought possibly Bamford got a slight touch to the ball.

Raphinha was involved in a good bit of play and in another move won the ball straight back after losing it. Raphinha then crossed the ball for Bamford to put the ball into the net, but it had already gone out of play. At one point we were too close for comfort when playing

across the back four, but I would rather play out from the back. A short while after it proved my theory when the ball was kicked long from Meslier but was immediately picked up by West Ham to put them on attack.

The game turned on its head when West Ham were awarded a penalty when Ayling caught their player. Meslier was very unlucky as he saved the initial penalty, but West Ham were quicker off the mark than our players and put the rebound into the net to give them the lead. Maybe our players just assumed they were going to score but West Ham being in the lead was against the run of play. Raphinha put in a good cross that was caught by their keeper. West Ham were awarded a free kick in a good position after a Cooper foul, with their players lining up to take the free kick talking behind hands and shirt seemingly so no one could lip read them. A deflection won West Ham another corner and they then scored from a header in between Llorente and Ayling after losing our markers just before the half-hour mark.

It was an end-to-end game, but luck had deserted us as they had another shot over the bar. There was no doubt in my mind that we would be making changes at half-time today as our midfield was non-existent with West Ham running through us easily at times. I was frustrated with our disallowed goal as that counting would have made a difference to the game. A long-range shot was put around the post from Meslier. With Ayling pushing up so far, he kept getting caught out on the wing when West Ham attacked us. Just before the whistle blew West Ham won another corner and saw the ball rebound off the post and cleared by us as Leeds went into half-time losing 2-0.

At the start of the second half Alioski and Harrison replaced Klich and Costa with Dallas moving into midfield with Alioski at left-back. An early cross from Leeds was easily caught by their keeper. A fantastic through ball from Llorente to Bamford was a great chance but went just wide and could have put us immediately back into the game had it gone in. Phillips ended up in the book, despite getting the ball first. A fantastic shot from Raphinha with his back to goal was tipped over the top from their keeper before a West Ham chance saw their shot come back off our crossbar. Raphinha was shining with another good run and his shot was narrowly wide. Rodrigo replaced Roberts with half an hour left as Leeds kept going forwards in an end-to-end game, with a great pass from Harrison to Alioski on the wing. His cross saw Raphinha's shot saved by their keeper. When Raphinha went to take a corner won by Rodrigo, the contrast to West Ham corners were noticeable. They constantly stood in front of Meslier piling pressure on our defence whereas we did not put any pressure on their keeper as he was surrounded by his own players.

After another Leeds corner did not come to anything, West Ham went on the counter-attack but Dallas got back to defend well. Another attack by them saw Llorente miss the ball and bring their man down to give West Ham a free kick in a good position on the edge

of the box, but luckily, they put the chance wide. Dallas made a good run forward but was unlucky with the final pass picked up by West Ham. Another great chance for Leeds to pull a goal back saw Bamford hit the ball over the top of the goal after a great pass from Raphinha. What a shame he could not put the ball in the net like he did in the first half when it did not count. We have got to take our chances and getting one goal back would have given us that chance to get something out of the game. They got booked for kicking the ball away as Leeds never gave up and were still attacking. Rodrigo had a shot over the bar when maybe Ayling was in a better place to the right of him, but he had to try. We only needed that chance, but West Ham got the luck as they cleared the ball off the line after a great cross from Ayling. They had a long range shot easily saved from Meslier before some strong play from Phillips saw his long shot well wide.

As the whistle blew for full time which saw Leeds lose in London, the hoodoo strikes again! We will have to learn to be clinical and put our chances away as in this division, you do not get a second chance at it sadly. With games coming thick and fast, the Chelsea game at Elland Road at the weekend will be an early lunchtime kick-off. Keep fighting Leeds as you did today, and it will come good in time.

LUFC – Marching on Together!

LEEDS UNITED V CHELSEA; 13 MARCH 2021 AT ELLAND ROAD

I had a stark reminder on Tuesday of the impact the power of love I have for following my team everywhere and our fans has on my well-being. Coming home from work and being down in the dumps had me feeling sorry for myself. Getting contacted by Natasha and Vicky to join them and Rhiannon on the AllLeedsTV Leeds United lasses programme that evening was the best tonic I could have had. I really enjoyed having the football banter and talking about Leeds United despite our loss the night before. Thank you for inviting me on to the show and for showing how great the Leeds United family are. The link to the recording is: https://www.youtube.com/watch?v=83mSHlAuCFQ

I would also like to thank Ken for buying my book *Leeds Are Going to the Premier League!* and as always, your support is appreciated.

I also started reminiscing as the reality of pretending I am 35 hits home as I prepare to retire from work in the summer. Fifty years ago, on leaving school, my friend Sue and I made a pact to see how many Leeds games we could attend without missing one. I then went seven years without missing a game home or away and went abroad to see the greatest Leeds team ever. I am sharing some of my photos of the young girl in a man's world, which takes me back to those days. Despite all the troubles and trauma of following my team in that era, I would not change it for the world. I was privileged to be there and to see Billy

Bremner lift the FA Cup in 1972. Going to both Salonika in 1973 and Paris in 1975 remain special despite the results. Following this team has made me the loyal Leeds United fan I am today.

Although we are playing Chelsea at Elland Road today, in 1971 I had told my mum I was going to see Leeds play at Stamford Bridge whether she liked it or not having told me I could not go to Southampton, the previous long-distance away game. I was working and earning my own money and my love affair of going to all away games too was born then and continues to this day. Abbey Coachways, my local coach company, only went to home games and the nearer away games at that time, so it meant we would have to travel to Leeds to go to games a long distance away.

Team: Meslier, Ayling, Struijk, Llorente, Bamford (making his 100th appearance), Alioski, Phillips, Dallas, Harrison, Raphinha, Roberts.
Subs: Rodrigo for Bamford (35), Costa for Harrison (64), Klich for Rodrigo (79).
Subs not used: Casilla, Koch, Poveda, Berardi, Shackleton, Jenkins.
The game ended in a 0-0 draw.
Attendance: Zero, behind closed doors.
Referee: Kevin Friend.
Booked: Roberts, Alioski and Rodrigo.
Bielsa made three changes to the team that played West Ham with Costa and Klich on

the bench, and Cooper not in the team. Phillips was limping in the first minute after a challenge but was able to carry on. Dallas playing in midfield made an early tackle letting Chelsea know they were going to be in a battle today. Chelsea nearly took the lead as the ball was pounced on the line by Meslier to stop it going in. Within 14 seconds a Leeds counter-attack saw Bamford pass the ball across to Roberts in the penalty area who blasted it into the net only to see it chalked off for Bamford being offside in the build-up. With things coming thick and fast it was Chelsea's turn to see us clear the ball at the other end only to see it rocket off Llorente, the rebound hit the crossbar and was then scooped up by Meslier. Back to the other end Roberts had another great chance only to see his shot pushed on to the woodwork from their keeper. Leeds were playing well, chasing after everything as Chelsea had another attack and straight away I shouted that it was offside. I did not see the flag go up at the end of the attack, but the comments were justified as I was proved right.

Roberts was booked for a challenge from behind as he studded the back of their player's knee as he was falling. With 25 minutes played, Chelsea were making us play deep across the back four which in turn invited them to attack us. As Struijk deflected the ball over for a corner, Chelsea looked to be getting a foothold in the game. Bamford was hurt in an aerial challenge as their player barged his hip and looked to be struggling as he hobbled about before going down injured. Eventually Chelsea put the ball out so he could get treatment. At that point I was not sure if he would come back on, but he did, although he did not last long and had to be subbed. Poor Bamford, a memorable game for his 100th but for the wrong reasons. Ayling's flop was quite theatrical as the referee waved play on. After a couple of Leeds attacks which won us a corner and a throw-in, another one broke down as Chelsea went straight to the other end in injury time and brought a save from Meslier to keep the score 0-0 as we headed into the break.

The commentators praised Leeds for playing 'Marching on Together' at the start of the second half to create an atmosphere. To have us singing it in the ground again will be awesome. With Raphinha on the attack in an offside position Chelsea won the ball back as the referee waved play on. Chelsea then came close to taking the lead two minutes into the second half but put the ball over the bar. Roberts had made some great running into space down the left-hand side, but his shot did not have enough power on it and was saved by their keeper. Rodrigo looked to have been moved to play deeper in midfield, with Roberts up front, but he was not as effective in that position as he'd been in the first half when he played higher up the pitch. That said, Rodrigo was involved with our next attack. Chelsea were upping the tempo but it was Leeds who came closest to scoring with a save on the line from Raphinha; their keeper reacting well, when he looked to be anticipating the ball at the near post. Roberts going forwards on the wing again was proving to be effective.

Although we were closing down as quickly as we could, it seemed we had lost our way a little as Chelsea brought a save from Meslier. They were through again but put the ball wide with Leeds players closing in to put him off. When Costa prepared to come on, I was already typing Harrison's name before a decision had been made. We need to be able to keep the ball up front more. As Raphinha was pulled up for a foul the commentators said he had caught their player in the face. Now that is funny, how can his arm be described as his face? The whistle blew for a free kick to Chelsea, but Ayling carried on forward only to end up on the floor in agony holding his knee. With a Chelsea player trying to drag him up, my concerns were that they were making an injury worse as I knew immediately Ayling was not pretending to be injured. He eventually walked off the pitch after treatment so fingers crossed, he will be okay.

As Roberts made another run forward, I was hoping a run in the team will do him good. When Alioski chased back after their player when our attack broke down, I knew he was going to get booked for the tackle as he went to the left of their player instead of the other side of him. A long-range shot was saved by Meslier, and stats showed they had had 14 attempts then to our four, so we were up against a strong team. Rodrigo found himself in the book too before the referee went straight over to have a word with Alioski seemingly saying he would be off if he did it again. I've no idea what happened at that point as it sounded like something had happened off the ball.

Leeds were putting pressure on Chelsea as we won a corner, then had a Llorente shot deflected for another one. Rodrigo was unlucky to see his header straight at their keeper saved by him at the second attempt. Klich was then brought on to replace Rodrigo which was a surprising sub to me even though I admit he was not doing too well playing in a deeper position. A bad clearance from Leeds had Chelsea back on the attack but even though it was offside, Meslier came out to the edge of the box and claimed it anyway. Our new pitch looked to be holding up well after all the recent rain and looks to have embedded better. Some of our players were wearing deeper studs too which will have helped them keep their footing better and there were hardly any slips in comparison to previous games. Roberts was pulled up for offside, but it looked like their far player was playing him onside to me. He was given the man of the match award, had played well, and was looking to prove me wrong for having said he was not a 90-minute man.

As we played the final minutes of the game, Chelsea had another shot in our penalty area which luckily was straight at Meslier who saved it. Some good defending from Struijk and then Alioski (who went down injured) saw Leeds keep them out and keep the game at 0-0. That was another thing proving me wrong as I had been saying we do not seem to get draws anymore but am more than happy for that to happen. One point is better than none and we did well to get something out of the game. It was a tough game today and Leeds United rose to the challenge. Getting a draw is what I consider to be a good point

under the circumstances so well done lads. With another Friday night game facing us back in London at Fulham, I loved it when we took over the neutral part of the ground as well. Getting Struijk back in defence with his height has proved effective for me and has also got us another clean sheet. Let's keep that up and get three points next time.

LUFC – Marching on Together!

FULHAM V LEEDS UNITED; 19 MARCH 2021 AT CRAVEN COTTAGE

I have a big thank you to say to The Square Ball. They shared a recording of Greavsie announcing my daughter's birth 30 years ago, live on air just after half-time, at our game at Highbury on 17 March 1971. I had not missed a game home or away for seven years and my husband rang Highbury and managed to get the announcement read out. It was also announced on their scoreboard too and it was a fantastic thing that my husband managed to get done.

Sadly, she was not celebrating her birthday here on earth but up in heaven, as she died suddenly at 17 days old from an undiagnosed heart defect. The Square Ball were not aware of this when wishing her a happy birthday but for me, I am grateful for the poignant memories as it keeps her memory alive. She also attended her first game at six days old against Crystal Palace the following week albeit in the crèche in the South Stand.

Team: Meslier, Struijk, Llorente, Phillips, Roberts, Ayling, Alioski, Harrison, Dallas, Raphinha, Bamford.
Subs: Klich for Bamford (77), Koch for Roberts (90+3).
Subs not used: Casilla, Berardi, Costa, Poveda, Gelhardt, Shackleton, Jenkins.
Leeds won the game 2-1 with goals from Bamford (29) and Raphinha (58).Attendance: Zero, behind closed doors.
Referee: David Coote.
Booked: Bamford, Phillips.

They ran straight at us from kick off and got a corner after a clearance from Alioski hit Struijk and their man got through. A great through ball from Llorente to Bamford nearly got us through at the other end and that was all in the opening two minutes. It was nice to hear Meslier, at 21 years old, get praise from the commentators for the number of clean sheets he had kept this season. Fulham had a good run through us but their final pass to the side was not good, so we got the throw-in. A Leeds attack saw passing between Alioski and Harrison who then sent a great pass for Roberts. When his cross was headed in at the far post by Ayling to put Leeds into an early lead the cheers went up only to see VAR once again stick the boot in and disallow it for offside. How I hate that thing!

Some good harrying from Harrison saw the ball go out for a throw. Roberts won a free kick in a good position which was taken by Phillips but blocked by their wall. We then came under pressure from Fulham who started forcing us back and nearly came a cropper when Alioski sent a long ball back to Meslier and nearly put us into trouble. Remember, Leeds, the best form of defence is attack. Bamford was injured in our next attack from a free kick. One thing I had noticed was how physical Fulham were and they got away with quite a few fouls in the opening minutes of the game. Raphinha then put the ball in the net again but this time I had no arguments as it was offside.

Replays showed that if we would have released the ball straight away in the build-up, it might just have counted.

Leeds had been chasing everything up until then, but Fulham started putting us under pressure. They won a free kick after Alioski let their man know he was there on the touchline and won a corner from it. Leeds were then dicing with death as we couldn't clear the ball then Meslier made a great save and with Ayling behind him, he cleared it off the line. Fulham were closing us down and not letting us have any room, but I am hoping our fitness will tell in the end. Roberts did well to keep the ball and not get shoved off it when surrounded by their players.

A good cross from Alioski put Fulham under pressure and the ball came back out for a throw. Alioski threw it to Harrison who sent a great ball over to the middle for Bamford

to hammer in and definitely put us into the lead just before the half-hour mark. Bamford then found himself in the book, but I think he was unlucky as he was trying to pull back from the foul. Bamford's goal meant that we had been involved in 90 goals this season. As I was trying to work out what they meant, it was explained that Leeds had scored 44 goals this season and conceded 46.

Fulham won a second corner which they equalised from when their player managed to outwit Ayling in the penalty area. Fulham then started to pile the pressure on as we messed about, with Struijk's short header pushed away by Meslier, and he then made a further great save to prevent Fulham taking the lead. The ball was just not running for us as we kept giving the ball back to Fulham and finally a save from Meslier brought their attack to an end. Roberts kept changing sides and won a free kick. Reed should have been booked already when he kicked out at Alioski after the ball had already gone out for a throw to us, but he got away with this too. Earlier when we were on the attack, he ran off with the ball as it went out for a throw to us to prevent us carrying on. Raphinha took a great free kick which had four of our players running in behind the wall, but it was possibly offside anyway if it had gone in. As the commentators said that Leeds fans do not like to hear any praise for Raphinha as they do not want to raise his profile with other clubs, my retort was, 'It's called gallows humour and we are taking the pi*s'.

As we started the second half on even terms at 1-1, Mitrović came on for Fulham and as he put his shirt on it showed he had bruises all over his back from cupping. Straight from kick-off Fulham forced us back, winning a couple of corners. They carried on pressing us, which made mistakes happen. When Phillips lost the ball, he got back in defence and forced their player over the line who then carried on down the slope and hit his head on the advertising boards. When Dallas got the better of their player, winning the ball back, he was brought down which earned a booking for Fulham. As Leeds won a corner, Fulham pulled everyone back in to defend it. We still managed to have three in quick succession with the third one after a great run from Harrison, which brought a save from their keeper that rebounded off their player. Fulham started attacking again and Dallas fouled their player. From their free kick, luckily their player fluffed his shot and Leeds won the ball and turned it into an attack. A great through ball from Bamford for Raphinha to run on to and take forward saw him slam it into the net on the hour mark to give us a second goal 28 seconds after their attack broke down. That is the Leeds way and I love it.

The game was not over yet though as Fulham shouted for a penalty after the ball hit Dallas. Roberts then made a late challenge but hurt himself in the process. With another late challenge on Raphinha which did not even get us a free kick, the ball was put out for him to receive treatment. At that point Ayling was stood at the side of the pitch not looking too good but had a pouch of something for energy. Leeds started to pile the pressure on after a great pass from Roberts saw Raphinha nearly through again, but he just could not get a shot in, and another chance went wide. With another tackle from behind on Raphinha, I could not believe that did not warrant a booking. Bamford eventually went down injured and was subbed for Klich with around 15 minutes left.

It was important we did not let Fulham back into the game when they won a corner straight after the substitution. Leeds cleared it and ran straight to the other end and won a corner themselves. The corner from Raphinha to Alioski at the edge of the box was a good move but he caught it wrong, and the ball went way over the top. A shot from Dallas went narrowly wide but it looked like the keeper had it covered, then some good work from Harrison won Leeds another corner. An Ayling header across the goal from the near post saw Harrison coming in at the far post but he could not get on the scoresheet. Klich saw his shot go wide and Alioski's shot was saved by the keeper. Leeds were digging deep into their reserves and battled to keep Fulham out with some great defending. As Leeds ran out of defence, Raphinha was brought down from behind again but this time it earned the Fulham player a booking. About time!

Koch replaced Roberts deep into injury time as Leeds prepared to battle until the end of the game. As Phillips kept hold of the ball when Fulham were awarded a free kick, he did not get the same leniency from the referee as the Fulham player in the first half and was booked. It was no different to what happened in the first half so why didn't their player get booked too? Just because Fulham were running out of time to get something out of the game perhaps. Well done Leeds as they fought until the end to win the three points and end our London jinx at long last. We now have a break until the Sheffield United game on 3 April so this should give our players time to recuperate as we took some knocks today.

LUFC – Marching on Together!

CHAPTER 8 – APRIL 2021

LEEDS UNITED V SHEFFIELD UNITED; 3 APRIL 2021
AT ELLAND ROAD

The day after my last blog, we received the sad news that Peter Lorimer had died after a long illness and again a few tears were shed. Rest in peace Peter and thanks for the memories, my thoughts are with your family and friends. Having been part of the Kop Committee to raise funds for your testimonial year, you created a special bond with us fans and this has carried on to this day especially with our Norwegian fans. Your goal in Paris means we will always be champions of Europe – WACCOE!

As the poignant dates of 4 and 5 April come around once again, alongside Peter's death, it was nice to see the club have a minute's applause before the game today and wear black armbands. The fourth sees the 30th anniversary of the sudden death of my baby daughter at 17 days old from an undiagnosed heart defect. The fifth sees the 21st anniversary of the murders of Christopher Loftus (Chris) and Kevin Speight (Kev) in Istanbul the evening before our game against Galatasaray. I was due to go to this game but was too scared to go having heard many stories about their fans beforehand; my fears happened in the most horrendous way and my thoughts are with Chris and Kev's families and friends at this sad time.

There has been some great fundraising going on with Leeds United fans raising monies for flowers for Chris, Kev and Peter from WACCOE and thank you to Mark Hutchinson for sharing his photos. Also, Kam Mann has raised over £4,000 for flags to be made for Chris and Kev with any remaining monies going to Candlelighters. Thank you to Kam for sharing his photos too. Well done to everyone involved and this shows once again that these lads will never be forgotten, and this keeps their memories alive. Adam Pope on BBC Radio Leeds also replayed the 20th anniversary recording with Andy Loftus, Gareth Senior and Alan Green after the game today. These are very harrowing memories from that horrendous night and shows why the lads should never be forgotten.

I was invited on to an Arsenal podcast this week by Tom Pheby who had found me on LinkedIn due to my match reports. I am looking forward to sharing the link in due course and it was good to talk about my passion as a Leeds United supporter with my favourite game being the FA Cup Final in 1972.

Team: Meslier, Cooper, Llorente, Roberts, Phillips, Dallas, Raphinha, Ayling, Alioski, Bamford, Harrison.
Subs: Rodrigo for Bamford (65), Klich for Roberts (81), Koch for Dallas (90+2).

Subs not used: Casilla, Hernández, Costa, Poveda, Struijk, Shackleton.

Leeds won the game 2-1 with goals from Harrison (12) and a Jagielka own goal (50).

Attendance: Zero, behind closed doors.

Referee: Graham Scott.

After a Leeds free kick where Raphinha's shot went over the bar, he was then on hand with a vital interception of a pass at the other end to put the ball out for a corner. With ten minutes gone a long-range shot from Phillips was spilt by their keeper but caught on the rebound and he then made another save from Dallas. Leeds then scored a brilliant goal shortly after which started with Llorente, then Roberts before some great footwork from Raphinha in the area to the byline, passed to Harrison at the far post to hit the ball into the net. Sheffield had a couple of attacks, a free kick and a long range shot that went wide before Leeds launched another attack. A cross from Ayling was headed out and Alioski's shot won Leeds a corner.

Leeds were awarded a free kick after a Sheffield attack but their player thought he should have had the free kick and moaned like hell. There was hardly any contact with him, so I am not sure of the reason why it was given. Roberts was then brought down with a bad challenge, but the referee played advantage. It looked like Harrison would get his second goal of the game, but the final ball was just wide. Although the referee and VAR said no further action was to be taken against the Sheffield player, it should have been a free kick and their player booked at least. With him coming off worse, it felt like him staying down gave him a reprieve. He was replaced just before half-time with a concussion substitution which is now allowed apparently. The commentators who stated it was not a nasty challenge between the two players need to open their eyes, as it was a bad foul on Roberts and their player is lucky not to have seen a red card. When play resumed, we had been given a corner so Harrison's shot must have been deflected. I feel this took the sting out of the game as their player was down for a while as at times it felt like a practice match.

Just before half-time the game picked up again as persistent work from Roberts and then Ayling saw Leeds win another corner. At the other end Leeds cleared the ball from a Sheffield corner but they won it back to send the ball across our area, before we ran forwards again and Roberts had a shot that skimmed past the outer post. Leeds battled to win the ball and came away with it only for their player to grab it deliberately to stop us going forward which earned him a booking. Sheffield got an equaliser right at the death when the ball came off the back of our player to their player at the far post. Although the shot was kicked out of the goal by Ayling the ball had already crossed the line. Whether we had switched off or not I am not sure but all of a sudden, they had a man down the right-hand side all on his own. With the final chance of the half Roberts saw his header easily saved by their keeper to keep the score at 1-1.

Photo courtesy of Mark Hutchinson.

Sheffield started on the attack in the second half seemingly coming out with a purpose and buoyed by that goal just before half-time. Some great play again from Raphinha left their player on the floor and Dallas then shot over. Roberts sent a fantastic ball to Harrison on the left and his cross was put into the goal by a Sheffield defender five minutes after the restart. Dallas saw another shot clip the corner of the crossbar and post. Roberts was playing well, and it looks like the run in the side was doing him good. It looked like he was playing in Klich's role today so maybe in a different position to normal? We had another good move which saw Alioski hit the ball high and over before another saw Bamford take a touch too many in the penalty area and they won the ball back. Llorente made a great tackle before an Ayling cross for Bamford brought a save from their keeper.

Sheffield counter-attacked and won a corner, but we won the ball back and broke out ourselves. Some great work again from Raphinha saw first his shot, then one from Alioski blocked. Great work from Ayling in defence saw him block their shot at the last minute to retain our lead. Rodrigo replaced Bamford who has had a quieter game today. Sheffield started to put more pressure on us and won a free kick even though their defender was behind Alioski, although replays showed he had caught him across the face. A poor pass from Phillips saw him chase Sheffield to get the ball back and brought their player down giving away a free kick. Leeds then broke away with four players going forward and Dallas's shot was just wide. Roberts was replaced by Klich before some end-to-end football saw the final ball from Harrison unable to get through to Rodrigo in attack. We had had 21 attempts so far in the game. Having given advantage first, the referee brought the ball back for the free kick and booked Rodrigo for a foul. I am assuming the difference to the foul on Roberts in the first half was because Sheffield lost possession. Sheffield had another free kick and then had a long range shot that went just wide. They tried again with another long range shot that did the same but luckily Meslier did not touch the ball, so we got the goal kick.

With five minutes time added on Harrison shot wide, then a great ball from Dallas to Raphinha saw Leeds win a corner. Koch made his first appearance since injury when he replaced Dallas and I wondered who he was at first. Rodrigo saw his shot saved by their keeper as the referee played over the five minute's injury time but finally the whistle went, and Leeds got the win and a welcome three points. As relegation looms for Sheffield United, Leeds moved into tenth place for the moment. With an away game at Manchester City before home games against Liverpool and man utd we are nearing the end of this season. Keep going Leeds, and let us start upsetting the apple cart a little please!

LUFC – Marching on Together!

MANCHESTER CITY V LEEDS UNITED; 10 APRIL 2021 AT THE ETIHAD STADIUM

Once the game kicked off, I was fine, but before that I wanted to cry. I just cannot get the same enthusiasm pre-game when I know I will not be at the game in person.

Team: Meslier, Cooper, Ayling, Phillips, Alioski, Bamford, Raphinha, Dallas, Roberts, Costa, Llorente.
Subs: Struijk for Bamford (45), Koch for Roberts (63), Shackleton for Raphinha (90+5).
Subs not used: Casilla, Poveda, Hernández, Berardi, Gelhardt, Klich.
Leeds won the game 2-1 with Dallas scoring a brace (42 and 90+1).

Photo courtesy of Mark Hutchinson.

Attendance: Zero, behind closed doors.

Referee: Andre Marriner.

Booked: Alioski.

Sent off: Cooper.

There was a two-minute silence as a mark of respect after the death of Prince Phillip, Duke of Edinburgh yesterday with black armbands worn by the players. I was looking forward to a good game but suddenly got extremely nervous, knowing we were up against a good team but feeling that we had to do well today. After having two magpies for good luck in my garden this morning, I was waiting to see if that worked in our favour.

Photo courtesy of Mark Hutchinson.

Photo courtesy of Mark Hutchinson.

A good run by Raphinha but his cross into the box was behind our player otherwise we could have been in a good position to score. Players from both sides were slipping all over the pitch in the opening minutes taking me back to how ours had been earlier this season. There were flashes from both sides in winning corners, but nothing came of them. Another great run from Raphinha saw him cross the ball in the box. Bamford was coming in behind the defender and thought he was getting the ball so was unprepared when it came through just behind him. What a shame as that would have been a good goalscoring opportunity. With City closing us down well there was not a lot of space to work with, but Costa kept going to win the ball. City attacked us again and two good blocks from their corner, first from Cooper and the second from Bamford kept them out. Costa again came away with the ball after some good work but seemed to slow up with a City player breathing down his neck.

Some nice defending from Dallas before some silly passing around the back four put us under pressure and in trouble, but luckily we got the ball away. We cannot afford to give the impetus to a team like City. A fantastic ball from Raphinha to Roberts ended with a corner to Leeds. Raphinha's corner did not beat the first man, so Phillips took our second corner, but nothing came of it. A back pass to Meslier saw the ball go under his foot but as he was far enough out of goal, he got to the ball in time to get it back again. A City attack saw Meslier save with his feet to keep the score at 0-0 then they won a free kick as their player went down easily with Roberts chasing him.

A foul on Bamford earned their player a booking but the free kick from Raphinha went straight to their man who cleared it. Meslier made the save from a low shot before City had another chance, but the final shot was wide. Phillips was battling to keep the ball when he received a kick, but the referee played on. He then spoke to Phillips who must have said something to him. The commentators said that Leeds had not had a shot on goal in the first 35 minutes. No, we had not, but on 42 minutes we were in the lead! Costa's persistence paid off as he got the ball to Bamford; he laid it off for Dallas to hit the ball off the inside of the post and into the net for Leeds to score. That was a good-timed goal to score just before half-time, but things turned on their head shortly after that. As City came back on the attack Cooper got booked but he had played the ball first. I thought that was an unjust booking even though their player stayed down. The referee then consulted with VAR and took back the yellow card only to give him a straight red card instead, as Cooper had caught their player's back leg with his studs. That was hard lines for Cooper as I thought the referee had rescinded the yellow card altogether, as momentum carried him forward after winning the ball. Bielsa made a tactical substitution then and brought on Struijk for Bamford. With three minutes' injury time to play, the referee played nearly six minutes, but why, I have no idea.

Photo courtesy of Kam Munn.

The second half saw their player fall down with hardly any contact and when we got a push in the back our player carried on. We were going to have 45 minutes of City attacks and would have to rely on breakaway attacks from Leeds. Good defending from first Alioski then Phillips putting the ball out for a corner kept up that siege mentality with our backs against the wall. A great save from Meslier saw him react quickly to get the ball at the second attempt. Their player stood on Meslier's hand when he had got both hands on the ball and did not even get pulled up by the referee for it! The difference with some of their players being wet blankets and going down at the slightest contact showed a lot. Meslier was catching the ball and commanding his area well as he made another save. Koch was brought on to replace Roberts before Alioski found himself in the book for a foul.

Meslier tipped the ball over the top from a long range shot then made another save shortly after. When City brought Foden on as sub, it did make me feel slightly anxious and my fears were true to form when they equalised. Their man was left on his own in the penalty area, but Meslier slipped just before their final shot to score. We had been mainly camped in our penalty area but had been man marking up until then. As there had been constant attacks from City, it was not surprising they had scored really. Leeds managed to win a free kick that Costa won and had Struijk and Llorente in their box, but City got the ball and raced forward to attack us. As our players raced back in defence their player was brought down to give us a reprieve as they were awarded a free kick. Alioski blocked a shot for a corner and then some good play from Phillips saw Leeds defending well.

Raphinha started to get forwards and was brought down which got them a booking. Shortly after this after a great ball from Phillips, Raphinha was through again with just the keeper to beat. As he tried to swap feet to shoot, the keeper won the ball with his feet to prevent Leeds taking the lead again. The last five minutes had seen the game opening up a bit as Leeds started looking for a winner. Phillips was awarded man of the match. Meslier made a save and then threw the ball straight out to the wing for Alioski to send a great ball through for Dallas. He ran forward and whilst battling with the defender, nutmegged the keeper to put Leeds back into the lead in injury time. I was screaming like a banshee as well as thousands of Leeds United fans around the world, as the team including Meslier celebrated in the right-hand corner of the pitch. What a goal Leeds and it looked as if it was going to be the winner.

When play resumed, Raphinha was through again but brought down with a bad foul that only got them a booking. I could not believe it when the referee once again had to play three minutes injury time but had already played five minutes. Apart from us scoring and celebrating, there was nothing that held the game up. With Raphinha injured in that tackle he was replaced by Shackleton for the final minute. With 96 minutes on the clock the referee blew for time and Leeds had won 2-1 and beaten the league leaders to go into ninth place in the table. After each minute of the second half dragging for so long whilst under attack from City, it was a great team performance and a ground out win.

What a morale booster that second goal from Dallas was as old habits die hard and every goal we score, gives cause for celebrations. I would have loved it even better in that

Photo courtesy of Kam Munn.

away end today though! The win today was dedicated by some fans to Chris and Kev as well as Pete Jenkinson from South Kirkby LUSC and Pudsey Macca who both died this week.

LUFC – Marching on Together in heaven lads.

LEEDS UNITED V LIVERPOOL; 19 APRIL 2021 AT ELLAND ROAD

As the news broke yesterday that Liverpool were one of the 'Big Six' clubs who have signed up to a European Super League, this has caused uproar amongst football fans all over the country. This is all about greed and money in a closed shop where no one can be relegated, and they still want their place in the Premier League. They have been moaning about too many fixtures already but want more games? Do not let them hold the power, if they want to go then let them, but they cannot come back.

Football is about supporting your team through thick and thin, which goes for all the little clubs too. Having already devalued the FA Cup which I hold dear, I still want the little

Photo courtesy of Kam Munn.

clubs to have a chance to beat the big teams. I also want promotion, relegation, something to fight for and the passion that goes with that. As it is, they have stuck two fingers up to their fans who I feel sorry for, as they are the lifeblood of football teams and without fans football is nothing. Shame on you!

Before the game I was interviewed by Arman from Canal+, the French rights holders for the Premier League, firstly on why Leeds is seen as the most hated club in England and secondly how Leeds fans are perceived by other fans clubs and why. I am looking forward to sharing this on my website when available.

Team: Meslier, Ayling, Harrison, Bamford, Struijk, Llorente, Phillips, Alioski, Dallas, Costa, Roberts.
Subs: Poveda for Costa (67), Klich for Alioski (79), Hernández for Roberts (86).
Subs not used: Casilla, Koch, Davis, Berardi, Gelhardt, Shackleton.
Leeds drew the game 1-1 with Llorente scoring the Leeds goal (87).
Attendance: Zero, behind closed doors.
Referee: Anthony Taylor.
Booked: Dallas, Alioski.

The Leeds team were wearing white t-shirts whilst warming up which said 'Football is for the fans'. As the game kicked off Orta was seen holding the same t-shirt up and there was also a big flag up in the Kop which said, 'Earn it on the pitch. Football is for the fans'. I could not believe my ears later in the game when the commentators said this was inflammatory from Leeds. So football is not for fans in their eyes? I will not say what my comments to them were!

As the game kicked off Liverpool were soon on the attack and through. Although I thought their player was offside, he lobbed it wide over Meslier and out for a goal kick. Meslier then was called upon to tip a long-range shot over the crossbar to keep them out. Leeds were trying hard to get the better of Liverpool but were overwhelmed with numbers or just couldn't get the final ball in. Roberts made a good run to keep the ball in, but the final cross was too long. Harrison and Costa were both unlucky to lose the ball and the latter could not get in a position to shoot. A great free kick saw Bamford put the ball wide, but the flag was already up for offside. Alioski made a great tackle in the penalty area after Llorente went down prior to that after he smacked his face when tackling the Liverpool player. Meslier then made another save when the ball came back into the penalty area.

Leeds were trying to play out from the back but kept getting into trouble which enabled Liverpool win a corner. A great cross from Alioski into their penalty area was put wide by their player. What a shame he did not do us a favour and put the ball into his own net.

Bamford was put through but as he took an extra touch, the ball was cleared for a corner. Dallas then took one for the team and was booked for a foul. After some cool play from Meslier in the penalty area, Liverpool took the lead a minute later with half an hour gone, when we lost their man and they scored after a through ball.

I felt we needed to look at our formation as there was something missing that was just not working out for us. Alioski found himself booked after our attack broke down and he fouled their player. Just then, Harrison passed the ball in the penalty area instead of taking a first time shot to catch them out. We were guilty of trying to go one step further than needed every time. Ayling was brought down with his back leg and earned their player a booking. Llorente then made a bad decision which nearly presented them with a second goal but luckily for us they did not get it. Just before half-time Roberts with our first real shot on target, saw it lack power and go straight to the keeper. As we went in at half-time losing 1-0 there was still a chance for us to get something from the game.

As the game kicked off for the second half Meslier made an early save. Struijk was pulled out on to the wing challenging their player, then Llorente put us into trouble again as the ball ran perfectly for Liverpool. At that moment I felt we needed changes but was not sure who or how but if Bielsa felt the team could do it, I would have to go with his judgement. It was nice then to see some good play from Llorente before a great cross from Alioski was put out for a corner. When VAR was brought in checking for handball, Mike Dean said it was not deliberate, so we did not get given a penalty, but I would have taken it. My shout of put some pressure on them Leeds and they will wilt, were because there looked to be a bit of panic on their faces when defending. We were getting in some good positions, but the final ball was lacking. As Llorente got the ball away he was fouled winning Leeds a free kick; from that a dangerous cross was put in, but we would have been offside anyway. Poveda was brought on and he brought a bit of a spark into the team. After some great play from Roberts at the edge of the box, he passed the ball to Harrison only for their keeper to deny him a goal, as he saved with his legs.

Leeds, and especially Roberts, were getting into the game more, winning two corners before a poor pass from Ayling saw Liverpool go on the attack. I lost patience with the commentators who were getting on my nerves as they were so far up Liverpool's backsides. Bamford was so unlucky not to score when his shot came back off the crossbar before Roberts got in a good position to shoot but the keeper saved. Liverpool counter-attacked with three against two and it was a relief to see Meslier get to the ball first at the other end. We could not get the ball to our players as Liverpool started to get back into the game. Klich was on in place of Alioski then Meslier found himself under pressure. Firstly, he sent a bad pass out that was picked up by Liverpool to win a corner. Meslier came for the ball then got back on his line tipping the ball over the crossbar for them to get another corner. Some good shielding from Phillips saw Leeds get the goal kick.

The cup file —
four steps on
the road back
to Wembley

It was lovely seeing Hernández come on to the pitch to replace Roberts with five minutes remaining as Leeds went on to win a corner. Harrison put in an excellent corner just out of reach of Bamford and Struijk only to see Llorente, in between three defenders, score from a header to equalise with three minutes of the game remaining. What a relief to see the ball go into the net, as it had been very tense because I was desperate for us to get something out of the game. The commentators were all over Leeds then, so two-faced! Suddenly with four minutes of injury time on the clock, it looked like Liverpool were going to get a winner and we had Meslier to thank for the vital save. When Llorente went down after a challenge, replays showed their player stand on him with his studs, but it was deemed not deliberate. As the whistle blew for a 1-1 draw, I was happy to see us put up a hard fight and not lose. Well played lads and let us upset the apple cart a bit more when we play that other red team from over the Pennines on Sunday.

LUFC – Marching on Together!

LEEDS UNITED V MAN UTD; 25 APRIL 2021 AT ELLAND ROAD

I have used my photos taken by the *Daily Express* in 1975 as they are a reminder of my love for Scotland due to the Leeds United players in the national team and of the Bay City Rollers. With lead singer Les McKeown dying suddenly this week, that is another part of my childhood favourites gone. My friend Linda who is in the photos with me said after a visit to old Trafford in the 1970s that man u fans had put our photo on a dartboard and thrown darts at us! The joys!

Last Tuesday I made an early morning appearance on BBC Radio 5 Live about my opposition to the European Super League. The whole thing collapsed very quickly after all the opposition from fans around the country, but I would not trust those six clubs as far as I could throw them not to try something like that again. These clubs need repercussions especially as Leeds United with our 'spying' at Derby resulted in a £200,000 fine for not acting in good faith. Even though we were in the EFL when that happened and not in the EPL, I would ban them from Europe for a period for starters. Those people excusing them points deductions because that punishes fans, it has not stopped the powers that be from doing that to other clubs before this. They cannot be treated any differently because they were supposed to be a 'Big Six' club.

I am glad the game was today rather than yesterday as I had an argument with my grandson Freddie's slide on Friday and came off the worst. After losing my balance, I went flying over it landing on my hand and bending my fingers back, it meant a trip to A&E. Luckily, although badly swollen and not being able to bend my fingers, I only sprained them. Although not back to normal yet at least I can use them to type again. As a neighbour observed it was a very spectacular sight albeit in my eyes, not like a dying swan but instead like a beached whale.

Team: Meslier, Alioski, Struijk, Llorente, Ayling, Phillips, Bamford, Dallas, Harrison, Roberts, Costa.
Subs: Poveda for Harrison (68), Klich for Costa (72), Koch for Roberts (76).
Subs not used: Casilla, Hernández, Berardi, Shackleton, Summerville, Greenwood.
The game ended in a 0-0 draw.
Attendance: Zero, behind closed doors.
Referee: Craig Pawson.
Booked: Ayling, Roberts, Alioski, Bamford.

I know many fans were looking forward to playing man u but to me it was just another game as I only concentrate on Leeds United. There again, as soon as I saw the kit, badge, and that awful colour on the pitch, I realised the dislike I felt for them was still underneath the surface with a passion. Some things never change. All I wanted was for Leeds to get something out of the game with a draw, but three points would be a bonus.

They got a free kick on the left-hand side in the first minute which brought an easy save from Meslier. This side proved to be very popular for the free kicks awarded their way as they put their next one over the top. I am not sure what had happened between Phillips and Fernandes, but something had them laughing together, maybe because Phillips was man marking him. Leeds then saw a shout for hand ball only to see VAR make a quick judgement on it and no penalty given, surprise surprise. Some of our passing lacked conviction but I thought we would get that once we settled down and would be fine. We were having to defend well as we were under constant attack apart from our little spell. When Harrison ran on to the ball on the wing, I assumed he had been judged offside when the referee stopped the game and gave the free kick to man u. He was well behind the defender though but when a similar thing happened shortly afterwards, I still had no idea why either of those decisions were given and wished they would have shown some replays of the incidents.

They were awarded a free kick on the edge of the box, but the shot went over the top. Leeds won our first corner just after the half-hour mark, but we could not beat the first man and they got the ball away. A good shot from Dallas straight at the keeper was saved by him. Ayling was closing Rashford down who was through on the wing and 'slipped' to bring him down which earned him a booking. Roberts then found himself in the book, but I thought he was unlucky to have been penalised. The referee was already getting me worked up with all the free kicks heading man u's way although when Struijk was pulled up, replays showed he did stand on James's foot. A fantastic save from Meslier kept it scoreless going into the break in what had been a very fast first half.

Harrison and Costa had swapped sides at the start of the second half. Leeds had to be on their toes when man u nearly got through, but we defended well and put the ball out for a corner. When their player went down easily in the penalty area and complained, replays showed some jostling with Alioski which never warranted anything further anyway. Leeds were letting them know they were there when our passing became crisper and we battled to come away with the ball. With our short passing between us that had them chasing shadows I knew the lads were doing well. A great through pass from Llorente started a move that ended with a great cross from Costa across the box, but no one was near enough to hit it into the net. With Phillips doing some great man-marking and then some excellent tackling from Ayling at the edge of the box, man u knew they were in a battle and some of their players did not like it.

Suddenly they were through on the attack again which brought a save from Meslier then Alioski whipped the ball off their toes just as they were ready to shoot. Leeds then went on the attack and a great shot from Costa won us a corner. Alioski then found himself in the book as they won the ball from Costa and started on the attack. As they were dropping like flies when being man-marked the referee obliged by giving them all the free kicks. When one lashed out at Alioski, I knew we were getting under their skins. Poveda replaced Harrison then Roberts was brought down which earned Maguire a booking. When Bamford kicked the ball away in frustration when he couldn't keep it in play, the referee booked him. Well, the same should have happened to their player in the first half then as he kicked the ball away after a free kick was given to us. The referee missed Costa being fouled and he had to go off injured just after that. That was not a surprise as us winning free kicks was definitely the rarer in the two teams.

Bamford sent a great through ball for Klich to make a shot, but it was quite tame and easily saved by the keeper who then saved a long-range shot from Ayling. Struijk was playing well and doing some great defending, but the ball was running better for man u as well as the referee giving them absolutely everything. The game was end-to-end with again good work from Struijk and Poveda. Their player was already trying to go down, but Poveda kept snapping at his heels and continued battling to keep the ball. My exasperation with the referee showed with my chosen words as he consistently gave every advantage he could to man u. In the final minutes we were battling to get the ball away but kept giving it back to them but eventually we were awarded a free kick on the edge of our box. As the final whistle blew and the score remained at 0-0, I was happy with that score. Well done lads, it was a good point and a battling performance and as always, I am proud to be Leeds.

With news coming out that Leeds fans can now pick up their crowdies I am looking forward to picking ours up once more dates are released. By the time I tried booking a slot they were all sold out very quickly and it will be so nice getting back to Elland Road. As the last few games are upon us Leeds were in ninth place with a respectable 47 points and have an away game at Brighton next week before Spurs at home the following week.

LUFC – Marching on Together!

CHAPTER 9 – MAY 2021

BRIGHTON & HOVE ALBION V LEEDS UNITED; 1 MAY 2021 AT THE AMEX STADIUM

As the COVID situation has had a severe impact on the sales of my last book *Leeds Are Going to the Premier League!* it is possible that my next book will be my last one. As it takes a lot of effort in writing my blog and turning them into books, maybe our first season back in the Premier League brings the books to a natural end. Although I will never be a salesperson, my marketing takes place at games and meeting up with fans in person.

Team: Meslier, Ayling, Llorente, Struijk, Alioski, Koch, Bamford, Dallas, Harrison, Roberts, Klich.
Subs: Poveda for Alioski (45), Rodrigo for Bamford (59), Hernández for Llorente (79).
Subs not used: Casilla, Berardi, Cody Drameh, Shackleton, Jenkins, Huggins.
Leeds lost the game 2-0.
Referee: Chris Kavanagh.
Booked: Ayling.

Finding out Phillips was injured with a calf injury just before the game kicked off was a blow. Koch on his return from injury would be playing in front of the back four alongside Klich. In one of our first attacks there was a foul from behind on our player, but no foul was given. Meslier was called into early action to make a couple of saves. Roberts was brought down on the wing and the resulting free kick taken by Harrison saw Klich win a corner. Brighton were then awarded a soft penalty against Alioski after he kept impeding their player in the box when trying to win the ball. Meslier was very unlucky not to save it as he guessed the right way, but there was too much power on the ball.

This is not a happy hunting ground for us here and recollections of us being 4-0 down at half-time a few years ago came to mind. The best thing about that game was the input from Leeds fans underneath the stands. Tony Winstanley's song, 'Oh Leeds United, I'm so delighted I chose you as my football team', had a global airing that day.

That penalty decision against Alioski seemed to have an impact on his performance. A good run from Dallas was put out for a corner which was taken by Harrison, but we could still not get the ball past the first man. Playing without Phillips is something we will have to work on as we were looking disjointed as a team.

Llorente took a long shot with their keeper off his line but although worth a shot, the ball went over the goal. Harrison's cross into the penalty area after some good work from Bamford saw Brighton come under pressure for the first time with a mix-up from their player and keeper. Harrison then had a shot saved by their keeper. With Bamford losing out on the ball on the goal line their keeper got the ball but had all the time in the world to take a kick as no one put him under pressure. Roberts had stayed back but as soon as he put the effort in a few minutes later, he won the ball back. Their player kneed Ayling in the face when he went to head the ball then tried dragging him up off the floor.

We were not out of the game yet as Harrison shot wide after a good build-up, but it felt like it was going to be one of those games today. Leeds continued attacking with first Alioski and then Ayling, after a good run down the wing from Dallas, winning corners. Another corner saw the ball come out to Roberts who saw his powerful shot blocked by their player on the arm. Dallas took a corner that brought an easy catch for their keeper. We really needed to make corners count especially when another one failed to make an impact.

Llorente went down after a challenge after receiving a boot on his ribs. To me Brighton were being very sly with their fouls but getting away with them. They won their first corner just before half-time and play was stopped as Leeds came away with the ball, even though their player went down after a challenge from his own team-mate. As he got up straight away there was no need to blow the whistle in my opinion. Brighton ended the half on the attack and could have put the game to bed. Leeds had tried playing out from the back, but Llorente was caught out as the ball was crossed in the box, but they put the ball over with

an open goal in front of them. Ben White ran the ball over the line after a long run and then they had another shot wide. Leeds tried coming forward again, but we had no end product. It was not a classic game by any means as we went in at half-time losing by that early penalty.

Alioski was replaced by Poveda at the start of the second half, but the first chance went to Brighton but was over the goal. Dallas had moved to left-back but as our midfield was not effective, we could have done with him there. Brighton were another team who looked to be raising their game to play us. Poveda was given a right push off the ball in the penalty area by their player, but nothing was said to him by the referee. The same challenge with less power won Leeds a free kick later in the game plus their soft penalty was given for minimal contact. What was the difference? Brighton came close to scoring again as Meslier came out and luckily got a touch to the ball to put it behind their attackers. After good work between Poveda, Roberts and Dallas the final cross was caught by their keeper. It was noticeable that Brighton had many giants in their defence but even though Ayling had a low shot, this was blocked too. They were also packing their defence with 11 men so it would need something special to get through them in one of those frustrating games.

Rodrigo, coming back from injury, replaced Bamford who had been given no support up front. His first challenge saw their player go down very easily and win a free kick. Brighton were still looking dangerous going forward and luckily Harrison blocked their shot but there

were shouts for handball; unbelievable as the ball hit his chest. They were in space again and shot wide. Some good play from Poveda saw him keep the ball whilst under pressure. Dallas was then nudged off the ball and given a free kick before their player was booked for a foul with 15 minutes left. Leeds were very unlucky with a Dallas shot just over the bar.

When Hernández was brought on, I could not believe it when Llorente was the player subbed. It did not have the impact Bielsa was looking for as Brighton were straight on the attack, we did not clear the ball far enough and they scored a second goal a minute later. Ayling then received a booking for blocking their player and not getting out of the way.

We had not played well today but Brighton had packed their defence to frustrate us once they had taken that early lead, so we were up against it even more. We did not have any answers to getting past them on a bad day at the races as the final score showed we had been beaten 2-0. It was a relief to hear the final whistle blow to put us out of our misery. Whatever happens we have done well with four games left until the end of this season, which has been unprecedented being played behind closed doors.

Whether it was the game itself that made me feel exhausted or the second COVID jab I had during the week, I am glad we have a week to recover before our next game. That is nothing compared to Phil Hay who has just had brain surgery to remove a benign tumour this week. I wish him a speedy recovery. Tuesday will see me finally visit Elland Road again to go and pick up our crowdies although I can find no details about the one, I did for my granddaughters. It will certainly pull at the heart strings being back there that is for sure.

LUFC – Marching on Together!

LEEDS UNITED V TOTTENHAM HOTSPUR; 8 MAY 2021 AT ELLAND ROAD

Having made my first return to Elland Road for ages to pick up our crowdies, I can honestly say that it certainly got to me, and I felt very emotional. As we are now in the ballot for the last game of the season against West Bromwich Albion, hopefully it will not be my last visit this season.

Team: Meslier, Ayling, Llorente, Struijk, Alioski, Bamford, Harrison, Roberts, Koch, Dallas, Klich.
Subs: Raphinha for Roberts (58), Rodrigo for Bamford (79), Phillips for Klich (90).
Subs not used: Casilla, Berardi, Shackleton, Poveda, Hernández, Davis.
Leeds won the game 3-1 with goals from Dallas (13), Bamford (42) and Rodrigo (84).
Attendance: Zero, behind closed doors.
Referee: Michael Oliver.
Booked: Koch.

With lots of heavy rain for hours prior to the game we will see how the 'Spurs' pitch holds up to the weather. As Phillips and Raphinha make the bench today after their recent injuries, Leeds have a strong bench today which was good to see.

Spurs won their first corner after five minutes then we saw some strong defending from both Llorente and Struijk at opposite sides of the pitch. The keeper was forced to save Bamford's shot after a great pass from Harrison and from a second corner Struijk's shot went over the bar. A good run from Roberts saw his shot ricochet off their player making it easy for their keeper to collect the ball.

Leeds took the lead on 13 minutes after a great cross from Harrison was nearly put into the goal from their player. This brought a save from their keeper, but Dallas blasted the rebound into the net for Leeds. Meslier was then called into action to make a save after a corner. Alioski was brought down with Leeds awarded a free kick, but the look on their player's face indicated he had done nothing wrong. Leeds did not have everything their own way as first Koch blocked a shot then some good play from Struijk got the ball away. There had been quite a few tackles from behind from the Spurs players, but they had avoided any bookings so far. Leeds were then caught out when Spurs equalised about ten minutes later as they went straight through us with just Meslier to beat. The ball ran for them as they got between two of our players with Alioski too far back to help.

A great run from Harrison ended with his shot saved by the keeper but our couple of corners did not come to anything. My heart sank when they put the ball into our net which would have put Spurs into the lead, but the flag had gone up for offside, thank goodness. When lines were put up on the TV and VAR looked at it, I knew it was going to be a tight decision as we have had fingernails go against us already this season, but consistency meant it was disallowed. We wasted a short corner before Harrison was pulled up when attacking the ball. Their player was already going down as Harrison put his arm across him to cross the ball. Their keeper got the ball anyway but there was nothing wrong with the challenge. A fantastic build-up just before half-time between Dallas, Roberts, Harrison and then Alioski saw the latter cross the ball from the byline for Bamford to score to put us back into the lead with a well-timed goal. This saw Leeds go in at half-time in the lead in what had been a great entertaining game.

It was good to see that the pitch had stood up well as Leeds were straight on the attack at the start of the second half. As Spurs were miles offside the linesman waited until Bale put the ball into our net before putting the flag up. Another great cross from Harrison saw Leeds win another corner before Koch took one for the team to bring Son down and earn a booking. Spurs had another chance after a ball from Struijk was picked up by them, but their final shot hit the side netting. Bielsa then decided to make an early change and brought Raphinha on for Roberts, moving Dallas into midfield alongside Klich. Prior to this Roberts had done some good work but was not quite clinical enough with his passes.

Struijk made a good block which won a corner for Spurs. Raphinha had straight away started to have an impact and was brought down which earned the Spurs player a booking. Leeds then started to pile pressure on Spurs, and I was screaming for us to take a shot after we were in so many great positions but had to contend with passing the ball between us. Eventually Klich hit a fantastic shot that was saved by their keeper. A free kick was awarded against Harrison which saw a good clearance from Alioski. Alioski was then brought down off the ball which gave us a free kick and their player a booking. Replays showed a deliberate arm from their player who was not even looking at the ball. Their player went down after being outfought by Struijk, but Spurs were awarded a free kick. Alioski, defending well, deflected the ball which brought a fantastic save from Meslier. Harrison was penalised for a foul just outside the box as he was running out from defence and their resulting shot hit the top of the bar. A good chance for Leeds was finally hit over the top by Harrison before a second chance for him shortly afterwards was blasted over the bar. He was playing really well but just couldn't keep those final shots down.

As Spurs came forward again Alioski was on hand to put the ball out for a corner. Meslier made another brilliant save to keep Spurs out before Rodrigo came on to replace Bamford. Alioski was playing really well as we saw more good defending from him. Klich was so close to scoring with another good chance. A great run from Raphinha saw him pass to Rodrigo in loads of space to crack the ball into the net and straight away he acknowledged the cross from Raphinha. As Raphinha received the pass I immediately thought he was offside but then thought no, their player at the far side was playing him on and VAR agreed with this decision.

With a 3-1 lead now, Leeds were determined to win the game as Ayling made a great block that sent the ball out for a throw. Phillips replaced Klich as Harrison was awarded man of the match by the commentators. Their keeper made a save from Dallas after he had a good lay-off from Rodrigo after an Alioski cross. Spurs got through our defence, but their final shot was well wide when it looked like a good chance as four minutes time was added on. Struijk blocked the ball as we battled until the end and the final whistle blew. That was a fantastic team performance, we had played very well, battled, got a great win and three points giving us 50 points in total. It was great to see another of the 'top six' teams finding out that we are up to the challenge. Well done, Leeds, as always, I am proud of you.

LUFC – Marching on Together!

BURNLEY V LEEDS UNITED; 15 MAY 2021 AT TURF MOOR

Well, it is never easy being a Leeds United supporter, is it? After entering the ballot for tickets for the last home game of the season it was gutting to find out that I had not been one of the lucky ones. Checking and re-checking my emails, logging on to the Leeds website to double check my account became a constant thorn in my side. It has taken me a good 48 hours to come to terms with this, even shedding a few tears as I felt so demoralised, plus I know that I am not the only supporter feeling this way. Following Leeds United has always been my respite that helps me cope, so I have really struggled since we have not been allowed to travel home and away to follow our team but have had to accept that I will not be at a game this season.

Many other fans were also in the same situation, but I feel sorry for those with an even better record of support than myself who have missed out too. For those who deride some of our fantastic supporters as being super fans who feel they are entitled to tickets, they would need to walk in their shoes to understand why they feel let down. Dedication and loyalty are something that we should all understand have brought about the fantastic worldwide fan base that Leeds United have. This is shown by their long records of going to games with some of them hardly missing any during a period from 20 to 50 years, which is an outstanding achievement and an even better record than I will ever have. They have gone to every game over the years which has involved Leeds United including home, away, friendlies plus pre-season tours abroad which became a way of life, and this is what should count, the number of consecutive games. Games which have involved very poor crowds over the years would see these fans in attendance regardless of how and who Leeds were playing. This is where the dedication and loyalty come in with never or rarely missing a game, so it is not just about who has supported Leeds United the longest.

That is not to deride any Leeds United supporter but to explain why missing a game has caused such an uproar. With having only 4,000 tickets for us, apparently being lucky in the ballot was made harder by not factoring any loyalty into our season ticket holders' applications. For some fans though tomorrow never comes, and details emerging on social media of two Leeds United fans having been diagnosed with terminal cancer, if any exceptions need to be made for them to attend then that should be the case. Good luck to those who have got tickets and I know I will be jealous not being there in person for the game but watching on TV instead.

Without any prompting from me though, it has been nice seeing and hearing the support from other fans for me to get a ticket (no, it has not made a difference) and I appreciate their comments. There may still be light at the end of the tunnel for a few more fans as yet. News has filtered through that some fans who won tickets in the ballot are not going to get their tickets for the WBA game so there is still a chance to be there, however small.

Team: Meslier, Ayling, Harrison, Bamford, Klich, Phillips, Llorente, Struijk, Dallas, Raphinha, Alioski.
Subs: Rodrigo for Bamford (58), Roberts for Klich (76), Poveda for Raphinha (81).
Subs not used: Casilla, Cooper, Davis, Shackleton, Berardi, Jenkins.
Leeds won the game 4-0 with goals from Klich (44), Harrison (60) and a brace from Rodrigo (77 and 79).
Attendance: Zero, behind closed doors.
Referee: Graham Scott.
Booked: Phillips.

I cannot wait to be back amongst our fans going to both home and away games and the photo was taken by me from our coach when travelling to Ipswich on 13 January 2018.

Leeds were put under pressure from Burnley in the first ten minutes with first Bamford putting the ball out for a corner then a good challenge from Llorente to win the ball for Leeds. The whistle blew for a free kick given to Burnley, but I must have missed what it was for. We had a few misplaced passes not reaching our players before Leeds settled into the game and started ramping up the pressure. Bamford forced a saved from ex-Leeds keeper Bailey Peacock-Farrell after it looked like he had lost the ball when he slipped in the penalty area but got up again and shot. Complaints were made from the Burnley players that when Bamford got up off the floor to shoot that he had fouled their player. Chris Wood and Charlie Taylor made up the Burnley ex-Leeds contingent.

163

Harrison was then penalised for offside which was a shame as it would have been a great opportunity. Dallas then had a shot on the turn that went over the top of the goal. Alioski missed the ball and fouled their man to give Burnley a free kick. Leeds went on the attack again and won another corner this time with a deflected shot from Dallas. Llorente required treatment after a knee in the back and was down for a while.

Alioski had a shot blocked then Raphinha was fouled, and a free kick given. We looked to get into some good positions for a long-range shot but kept passing the ball around as we tried to find a way through their defence. An excellent cross from Llorente saw another corner given. After some sustained pressure from Leeds, Burnley made a break but were stopped by the Leeds defence. As they tried attacking again, some good defending from Raphinha forced Taylor's attack over the line for a throw in. As Leeds came forward again, a challenge from Taylor in the box whipped the ball off Raphinha's toes giving Leeds another corner. After a short corner, a great cross in from Phillips was headed just wide from Struijk.

Bamford put the keeper under pressure but luckily did not foul him. Leeds were getting more and more into the game after coping with the early pressure. Alioski had a great chance but completely mishit the ball which went out for a throw-in. Whether it would have been classed offside in the build-up I am not sure, but it would have been a close decision. Raphinha hit a shot with his back to the goal but with Klich coming in behind him, he would have been in a better position to score. Meslier was quick off the mark to catch the ball and then in a typical move out of defence, Leeds scored a great goal just before half-time. Raphinha made a great run and then passed the ball to Klich in the middle of the pitch who ran forward and hit a fantastic curling shot past the keeper.

Burnley were straight away moaning at the referee about their player getting tangled with ours at the edge of our box before we broke away to score. Struijk was penalised for a free kick to Burnley at the end of the two minutes added on which was saved by Meslier to keep our lead.

Bamford and Tarkowski tangled off the ball at the start of the second half, but the referee let play go on. Ayling made a little contact on Wood then stood off him as he fell to the ground before Burnley had a shot that went wide. Wood should then have been pulled up for a foul by backing in to Llorente, but he was allowed to carry on and only a great save from Meslier to put the ball wide with his legs prevented an equaliser. Burnley then had another shot over the crossbar. Rodrigo replaced Bamford with over half an hour remaining and shortly afterwards there was no foul given with a Burnley player piggy backing our player. Leeds made a counter-attack and their defender just got in front of Rodrigo to put the ball out for a corner. Just after our first substitution was made, an Alioski shot was diverted into the goal from a Harrison back heel to give Leeds a second goal.

To me Wood was trying to con the referee by diving at the edge of our box, pushing Llorente about, and needed pulling up for it. Phillips then found himself in the book as Burnley had another shot wide. Raphinha was brought down and Westwood who fouled him was going nuts. The referee had the yellow card out, but he was allowed to remonstrate with Raphinha even though replays showed he did commit a foul. He should have still been given the yellow card but then a red card as well! I found all the spitting from the Burnley subs coming on to the pitch off-putting. The next thing the fourth official was speaking with the referee, Bielsa and Dyche at the side of the dugouts. With no one knowing what had happened, Ayling was called over to be spoken to with Alioski. After Alioski had been fouled their player had a go at him whilst still on the floor. The cameras then showed Alioski stick his tongue out and put both hands behind his ears. What a load of cry-babies Burnley have been today, they can dish it out but did not like things not going in their favour. Meslier made another great save with his feet for another corner to Burnley.

Bielsa made another substitution with Roberts replacing Klich with 15 minutes remaining. Within a minute Leeds had scored again with a great goal from Rodrigo which he lifted over the keeper after a fantastic through ball from Harrison. Two minutes later some more fantastic play from Harrison to Rodrigo saw the latter round the keeper to score again to put Leeds 4-0 up. There you go Burnley; football talks and cheating is for losers!

Our final substitution saw Poveda replacing Raphinha. It was nice to have Lucy Ward, ex-Leeds, commentating the game as I can cope with her good analysis of the game. Burnley had a chance from a corner although the narrow angle was covered by Meslier before putting more pressure on us. Meslier was fouled and a free kick given but the Burnley player tried claiming for a penalty; give me strength. A fantastic ball from Alioski to Rodrigo saw him stopped from claiming his hat-trick just as he was about to shoot. Replays showed Taylor did not even touch the ball so it should have been a penalty, but VAR didn't give it, so a corner was given instead. With three minutes added on Roberts sent a hard shot straight at the keeper after their player was hanging on to Rodrigo when he got past him. I do not think it was a case of the referee playing on but ignoring a few fouls on our players.

As the whistle blew, once again it showed an excellent display from Leeds United giving us a great victory and another three points. With just two games to go until the end of the season Leeds have done as I predicted at the start of the season: Aimed for the top!

LUFC – Marching on Together!

SOUTHAMPTON V LEEDS UNITED; 18 MAY 2021 AT ST MARY'S STADIUM

Wednesday, 16 May 1973. It does not seem so long ago that I was travelling to Greece for my first European away trip to follow Leeds to the European Cup Winners' Cup Final in Salonika. The injustices of losing the game with a bribed referee in place means that I still will never forgive or forget what happened that night. The Greeks in the ground at the end of the game were fantastic with their support of Leeds as they were already aware of the bribe that had taken place whereas us Leeds fans were not. We were in an open-air stadium, all sat on the large stone steps in a torrential downpour and the only dry patches were where we had been sitting. After the game, the Greeks were clamouring for any Leeds memorabilia, so I hung my scarf out of the coach window for a group to fight over and I am glad I had the opportunity to be there.

As I have missed out on tickets once again in the second ballot for the West Brom game, it was good to see a few fans who had not missed a game for at least 40 years being successful this time around. It will be good to get back to normal next season and have my season tickets in place because I know if I must apply for any, then I am never successful. Whilst it will be weird seeing fans back in the ground at Elland Road, I am sure the atmosphere will be second to none as we show other fans how it should be done.

Seeing Alioski's gesture from our game at Burnley has been reported, I despair that other people did not see it as a childish reaction of blowing raspberries at their player but was seen to be something else. With Koch and Klich given early leave due to their forthcoming involvement in the European Championship playing for their countries, I am glad that they both ended the season on a high with an excellent performance. Bielsa had made three changes to the team today with Casilla, Cooper and Rodrigo starting the game. This will also be the first game since Christmas with fans in attendance although no away fans were allowed, only 8,000 Southampton fans.

Team: Casilla, Cooper, Ayling, Llorente, Phillips, Bamford, Raphinha, Rodrigo, Dallas, Harrison, Alioski.
Subs: Berardi for Llorente (45), Struijk for Phillips (45), Roberts for Rodrigo (79).
Subs not used: Meslier, Hernández, Davis, Shackleton, Jenkins and Poveda.
Leeds won the game 2-0 with goals from Bamford (73) and Roberts with his first Premier League goal (90+4).
Attendance: 8,000 Southampton fans.
Referee: Peter Bankes.
Booked: Phillips, Struijk, Dallas.

Southampton put Leeds under pressure from the off with Casilla making a good save within the first couple of minutes. Vital defending from Phillips saw the ball deflect off their player, forcing Casilla to make the save, but the flag went up for offside anyway. Southampton, buoyed by their fans in attendance and because they were playing Leeds, had upped their game. With one of their players and Llorente challenging for the ball, although there was no shoulder charge the referee gave a free kick because their player went down. Cooper, defending well, put the ball out for a corner. When Leeds won a corner around the 15-minute mark, the stadium was deathly quiet despite fans being there. When Harrison challenged for the ball and their player stayed down, the commentators were saying it was a definite booking, but no card was shown.

Southampton attacked and with their player nearly through, Casilla had come out of goal, but the ball was eventually cleared by Cooper. A great cross from Harrison was cleared for a throw to Leeds before an Ayling shot was well wide. With the team playing 3-3-3-1 it felt like Bielsa was trying to experiment with a different formation. Another good move saw a Harrison cross back headed from Raphinha to Dallas who shot wide. It will come, Leeds, it will come. Phillips took a Leeds corner, but Llorente's header was wide. Although it had been a quiet 30 minutes so far with the formation not really working for me, Bielsa had to try something different sometime. Southampton tried claiming for a penalty against Harrison, but nothing was given.

Casilla's distribution was different to Meslier although he had not done anything wrong, but the first half hadn't been great so far. Llorente was hit off the ball but when play stopped their player was not booked but Phillips was for an earlier foul. Another save from Casilla put the ball out for a corner and then they shot over the bar. Rodrigo shot wide before Southampton attacked again with the ball bouncing across our area just missing their players. It was noticeable that their players were falling down at the drop of a hat but with one minute time added on, the scores were level at half-time.

My thoughts were that Bielsa would change things at the start of the second half and Berardi, making his Premier League debut, and Struijk came on to replace Llorente and Phillips respectively. Southampton were awarded a free kick in a good position outside the area and the ball hit the angle of the crossbar and post. Leeds started to step up the pressure with first Dallas having a shot saved by the keeper then we were unlucky with another couple of shots blocked. When their player went down in our penalty area, my heart sank but then handball was given against them. Southampton tried again when their player was hardly touched, but he went down like a sack of potatoes that looked like a dive and a free kick was given just to the left of our box. Their player looked up to see what the referee had given and then stayed down.

Bamford was unlucky not to score when he rounded their keeper, but the ball was put out for a corner. As the keeper caught him, the commentators said that if Bamford would have gone down it was a penalty, also saying Bielsa would not be happy with him. They do not know Bielsa then! Bamford went to head the ball after good work from Harrison then collided with their player. The trainers came on to the pitch as Bamford required plenty of treatment and was down for a while. The Southampton players looked to be diving all over the place. Good defending from Ayling and then when our attack broke down, Struijk was booked as he stopped their player from running out of defence. Some great play from Raphinha once again saw him cross to Alioski who shot straight at the keeper who saved it.

Dallas hit a shot over the crossbar before Leeds took the lead. A great goal from Bamford after beating the offside trap saw him put the ball through the keeper's legs with 18 minutes left. I knew he would not want to go off earlier when he was injured as he made a record with that goal. Bamford will become only the fourth Leeds player to register ten away goals in the Premier League in a single season.

Southampton had a long-range shot put wide by Casilla and their corner came to nothing. Some great skill from Raphinha saw his final shot over the bar though it was not far off target. Roberts replaced Rodrigo as it was noted how poor the atmosphere from the Southampton fans was. Raphinha put the ball into the net, but Bamford had been flagged offside in the build-up. Some nice play from Roberts saw him brought down and a free

kick awarded to Leeds before Southampton had another couple of shots, one wide and another over the top. With six minutes' time added on Southampton made a final push for an equaliser with a shot on the turn that looked to be on target but was well wide in the end. Cooper was then penalised, and a free kick awarded to Southampton. Straight out of defence from this with a fantastic throw from Casilla to Raphinha, he passed to Roberts who could not get his shot in. The ball came to Bamford who had a great shot saved by their keeper; when the ball came back out to Roberts, he scored his first Premier League goal deep into injury time to give us a two-goal cushion.

Struijk had received treatment from the trainers and went off to the side of the pitch. The final attack from Leeds saw a great run from Harrison, then Bamford, before Raphinha shot only to see it saved by their keeper. Leeds pulled the game around in the second half which gave them another three points guaranteeing a top-half finish. Being in eighth place after the game was a great achievement in our first season back in the big time. Although I did not expect anything else, Leeds have done us proud. With the final game of the season upon us and with some fans back in the ground, this will be the first game Leeds have played in front of a crowd since our win against Huddersfield on 7 March 2020.

LUFC – Marching on Together!

LEEDS UNITED V WEST BROMWICH ALBION; 23 MAY 2021 AT ELLAND ROAD

With the news that the final game of the season today marks the last one for both Pablo Hernández and Gaetano Berardi as Leeds United players, it was going to be emotional. With fans back in the stadium for the first time since the COVID-19 outbreak, at least they would make some noise to give the lads a good send off. We would be joining them after being lucky to get tickets in the third ballot. Thank you, Paul, for buying my book *Leeds Are Going to the Premier League!* After a quick trip to the Peacock it was good to catch up with Dave who I had not seen for many a year – he travelled with a group of us to Celtic for a friendly on 11 February 1976. Sorry I could not catch up with some of you in the lower part as I had to move on.

Although the queues were very long outside the Kop, the queue went down very quickly with us first having to show our tickets and the questionnaire email, before showing our ID at the entrance. The group in front of us going into the West Stand were having their tickets scanned but the scanner said they did not exist. After a short while this was rectified, and everyone got inside without further issues. The West Stand was initially not being used for the game but the upper part where we were had been filled. With wooden seats still there, it is not a surprise that the West Stand is overdue for renewal. To say we were in the corner too, there was a very strong cold wind.

Team: Casilla, Ayling, Alioski, Berardi, Cooper, Phillips, Harrison, Rodrigo, Raphinha, Dallas, Hernández.

Subs: Bamford for Rodrigo (45), Struijk for Berardi (70), Roberts for Hernández (70).

Subs not used: Meslier, Shackleton, Poveda, Casey, Davis, Jenkins.

Leeds won the game 3-1 with goals from Rodrigo (17), Phillips (42) and a Bamford penalty (78).

Attendance: 8,000 Leeds fans.

Referee: David Coote.

Booked: Phillips.

It was good to hear the fans singing 'Marching on Together' alongside the music as the team came out on to the pitch. Despite all the social distancing in place, there was a good atmosphere. West Bromwich came close in the opening minutes before Leeds took what we thought was an early lead. After a good attacking run, Hernández passed across the box where Rodrigo's pass was met by Harrison who put the ball into the net, only to see this chalked off for offside.

We did not have too long to wait for a goal as Raphinha won a corner for Leeds which he took himself. Rodrigo was waiting at the far post to head the ball into the net to put Leeds into the lead in front of the cheering fans. The team were making some good runs and displaying some great attacking football. Raphinha, back in defence, made a vital challenge as WBA tried to get back into the game. It was lovely seeing both Hernández and Berardi playing well and eventually after initially having some fans singing the old version of the song, both heard their names sung by the fans. 'Pablo Hernández, Pablo Hernández, Pablo Hernández plays for United with Gaetano Berardi. Gaetano Berardi, Gaetano Berardi, Gaetano Berardi plays for United with Pablo Hernández.' Just before half-time Hernández was fouled and won Leeds a free kick just outside the box. Phillips hit a great shot into the net from the free kick to score his first Premier League goal as Leeds went into the break with a two-goal cushion. Happy 60th birthday, Martin, and thanks for the photo.

Bamford was brought on for the start of the second half in place of Rodrigo. Hernández was doing his best to score a final goal for Leeds, but the WBA keeper saved both his shots. Berardi too tried getting on the score sheet alongside Ayling but both were unlucky. WBA decided to up their game and we were very lucky to see the ball eventually go past the outside of the post. That was a little too close for comfort, but it was good to see how relieved the players were as they had a laugh between them. When the trainer called for Struijk and Roberts to come back from warming up, we realised that there was going to be a double substitution and that Berardi and Hernández were going to come off together. It was very emotional seeing the hugging from the rest of the team with Alioski in tears as both players made their way off the pitch to a standing ovation. Thanks for everything lads and you will never be forgotten, having been part of our Championship promotion last season.

Eight minutes later Leeds won a penalty for handball and my first thoughts were that Hernández would have taken it if still on the pitch. As it was Bamford stepped up to score his 17th goal of the season, giving him a fantastic record for our first season back in the Premier League. With Leeds in full control and despite some pressure from WBA, it took a mistake from Leeds for them to pull a goal back on 90 minutes. In added time Phillips went down holding his shoulder after a challenge and needed treatment. As the whistle blew for full time, Leeds have had a fantastic season with a credible ninth place. Marcelo Bielsa and the team have made an impact with some fantastic attacking football, having pride in the shirt, and never giving up, giving Leeds fans a season to be proud of.

I look forward to having everything back to normal at the start of next season with full crowds in attendance. For those of you who look forward to my blogs and photos, thank you once again for your support and I appreciate your comments. To all of those I spoke to today, it was great to talk, and I look forward to catching up with you again.

LUFC – Marching on Together!

CHAPTER 10

STATISTICS FOR 2020/21

DATE	OPPOSITION	VENUE	COMPETITION	SCORE (home team first)	ATT	SCORERS
12.9.20	Liverpool	Anfield	Premier League	4-3	Zero – behind closed doors	Harrison 12 Bamford 30 Klich 66
16.9.20	Hull City	Elland Road	Carabao Cup second round	1-1 (8-9 on penalties)	Zero – behind closed doors	Alioski 90+3
19.9.20	Fulham	Elland Road	Premier League	4-3	Zero – behind closed doors	Costa 5, 57 Klich penalty 41 Bamford 50
27.9.20	Sheffield United	Bramall Lane	Premier League	0-1	Zero – behind closed doors	Bamford 88
3.10.20	Manchester City	Elland Road	Premier League	1-1	Zero – behind closed doors	Rodrigo 59
19.10.20	Wolves	Elland Road	Premier League	0-1	Zero – behind closed doors	
23.10.20	Aston Villa	Villa Park	Premier League	0-3	Zero – behind closed doors	Bamford hat-trick 55, 67, 74
3.11.20	Leicester City	Elland Road	Premier League	1-4	Zero – behind closed doors	Dallas 48
7.11.20	Crystal Palace	Selhurst Park	Premier League	4-1	Zero – behind closed doors	Bamford 27
22.11.20	Arsenal	Elland Road	Premier League	0-0	Zero – behind closed doors	
28.11.20	Everton	Goodison Park	Premier League	0-1	Zero – behind closed doors	Raphinha 79

5.12.20	Chelsea	Stamford Bridge	Premier League	3-1	2,000 Chelsea fans	Bamford 3
11.12.20	West Ham	Elland Road	Premier League	1-2	Zero – behind closed doors	Klich penalty 6
16.12.20	Newcastle	Elland Road	Premier League	5-2	Zero – behind closed doors	Bamford 35 Rodrigo 61 Dallas 82 Alioski 85 Harrison 88
20.12.20	man utd	Old Trafford	Premier League	6-2	Zero – behind closed doors	Cooper 42 Dallas 73
27.12.20	Burnley	Elland Road	Premier League	1-0	Zero – behind closed doors	Bamford penalty 5
29.12.20	West Bromwich Albion	The Hawthorns	Premier League	0-5	Zero – behind closed doors	Sawyers own goal 9 Alioski 31 Harrison 36 Rodrigo 40 Raphinha 72
2.1.21	Tottenham Hotspur	Tottenham Hotspur Stadium	Premier League	3-0	Zero – behind closed doors	
10.1.21	Crawley	People's Pension Stadium	FA Cup third round	3-0	Zero – behind closed doors	
16.1.21	Brighton	Elland Road	Premier League	0-1	Zero – behind closed doors	
26.1.21	Newcastle	St James' Park	Premier League	1-2	Zero – behind closed doors	Raphinha 17 Harrison 61
31.1.21	Leicester	King Power Stadium	Premier League	1-3	Zero – behind closed doors	Dallas 15 Bamford 71 Harrison 84
3.2.21	Everton	Elland Road	Premier League	1-2	Zero – behind closed doors	Raphinha 48

8.2.21	Crystal Palace	Elland Road	Premier League	2-0	Zero – behind closed doors	Harrison 3 Bamford 52
14.2.21	Arsenal	Emirates Stadium	Premier League	4-2	Zero – behind closed doors	Struijk 58 Costa 68
19.2.21	Wolves	Molineux	Premier League	1-0	Zero – behind closed doors	
23.2.21	Southampton	Elland Road	Premier League	3-0	Zero – behind closed doors	Bamford 47 Dallas 78 Raphinha 84
27.2.21	Aston Villa	Elland Road	Premier League	0-1	Zero – behind closed doors	
8.3.21	West Ham	London Stadium	Premier League	2-0	Zero – behind closed doors	
13.3.21	Chelsea	Elland Road	Premier League	0-0	Zero – behind closed doors	
19.3.21	Fulham	Craven Cottage	Premier League	1-2	Zero – behind closed doors	Bamford 29 Raphinha 58
3.4.21	Sheffield United	Elland Road	Premier League	2-1	Zero – behind closed doors	Harrison 12 Jagielka – own goal 50
10.4.21	Manchester City	Etihad Stadium	Premier League	1-2	Zero – behind closed doors	Dallas 42, 90+1
19.4.21	Liverpool	Elland Road	Premier League	1-1	Zero – behind closed doors	Llorente 87
25.4.21	man utd	Elland Road	Premier League	0-0	Zero – behind closed doors	
1.5.21	Brighton	Amex Stadium	Premier League	2-0	Zero – behind closed doors	

8.5.21	Tottenham Hotspur	Elland Road	Premier League	3-1	Zero – behind closed doors	Dallas 13 Bamford 42 Rodrigo 84
15.5.21	Burnley	Turf Moor	Premier League	0-4	Zero – behind closed doors	Klich 44 Harrison 60 Rodrigo 77, 79
18.5.21	Southampton	St Mary's Stadium	Premier League	0-2	8,000	Bamford 73 Roberts 90+4
23.5.21	West Bromwich Albion	Elland Road	Premier League	3-1	8,000 Leeds fans	Rodrigo 17 Phillips 42 Bamford pen 78

FINAL PREMIER LEAGUE TABLE

POS	TEAM	P	W	D	L	F	A	GD	PTS
1	MANCHESTER CITY	38	27	5	6	83	32	51	86
2	MANCHESTER UNITED	38	21	11	6	73	44	29	74
3	LIVERPOOL	38	20	9	9	68	42	26	69
4	CHELSEA	38	19	10	9	58	36	22	67
5	LEICESTER CITY	38	20	6	12	68	50	18	66
6	WEST HAM UNITED	38	19	8	11	62	47	15	65
7	TOTTENHAM HOTSPUR	38	18	8	12	68	45	23	62
8	ARSENAL	38	18	7	13	55	39	16	61
9	**LEEDS UNITED**	**38**	**18**	**5**	**15**	**62**	**54**	**8**	**59**
10	EVERTON	38	17	8	13	47	48	-1	59
11	ASTON VILLA	38	16	7	15	55	46	9	55
12	NEWCASTLE UNITED	38	12	9	17	46	62	-16	45
13	WOLVERHAMPTON WANDERERS	38	12	9	17	36	52	-16	45
14	CRYSTAL PALACE	38	12	8	18	41	66	-25	44
15	SOUTHAMPTON	38	12	7	19	47	68	-21	43
16	BRIGHTON	38	9	14	15	40	46	-6	41
17	BURNLEY	38	10	9	19	33	55	-22	39
18	FULHAM	38	5	13	20	27	53	-26	28
19	WEST BROMWICH ALBION	38	5	11	22	35	76	-41	26
20	SHEFFIELD UNITED	38	7	2	29	20	63	-43	23

FINAL COMMENTS

As the season has now ended, news coming out of the club means that they are not using Fullerton Park for the new Parklife scheme. This will now relocate to the Matthew Murray site where the new training ground was to be built. This means that there is plenty of space behind the West Stand for when the rebuild goes ahead. Thorp Arch stays in place for training for now and the club will look for new facilities in due course.

Leeds players have headed to the European Championship with Meslier (France), Koch (Germany), Phillips (England), Alioski (Macedonia), Llorente (Spain), Klich (Poland) and Cooper (Scotland) being called up to represent their countries. It is a long time since we have had that many from our team playing for their country. The great Don Revie side was a team of international players and my friends and I plus many other Leeds fans all followed Scotland because of the number of our players in the team. I do not really follow the international games anymore since the 1970s, but I made time to watch the final between England and Italy, which England lost on a penalty shoot-out, sadly. We used to attend all the home internationals back in the day before they were stopped, and it always made the close season pass quickly.

Alioski has left Elland Road after his contract expired and has joined Al-Ahli in Saudi Arabia. Casilla has now left on a season-long loan to La Liga club Elche and Leeds have signed goalkeeper Kristoffer Klaesson from Norwegian club Vålerenga as backup for Meslier. Leeds have signed Junior Firpo from Barcelona, a left-back, so I am looking forward to seeing him play.

Because of the late start to last season, which only finished at the end of May, the fixtures are out for next season and see Leeds with a tasty opening game at Old Trafford. Because of the new pitch being laid, Leeds had asked to play their first game away, but it would be nice to kick off the new season with this being the opening game for all away fans to attend too. Football is nothing without fans so get us back to games and give us our lives back please.

After attending a legends tour with Allan Clarke, Paul Reaney and Eddie Gray last week, it was a great event. I could listen to them all for hours and the Allan and Paul show was hilarious. The next day we heard the sad news from Elland Road that another of our legends from the great Don Revie side had died. Mick Bates was an integral member of that side with his loyalty and commitment shown. I know he has been ill for some time and my thoughts are with his family and team-mates. Mick, like all the other players in that team, had a great rapport with us fans. He lived in Sykehouse and I lived in Carlton, both near Goole. When the troubles on the terraces at away games were at their peak, he arranged for my friend Sue and I to pick up some complementary tickets at Newcastle. I last saw him

with Eddie Gray at the Plantation when the SLI were raising funds for Don Revie's statue. I will never forget his kind words of encouragement, telling me I should write my first book, *Follow Me and Leeds United*. Rest in peace Mick, you will never be forgotten. Terry Cooper has also died which knocked me for six despite knowing he has been ill too. With more tears shed, it is a sad day for his family, teammates, and those of us fans who were lucky to have seen the greatest team on earth. We used to call into his sports shop when we used to walk to the ground, and he always made time to talk to us. Seeing a photo of Terry and Norman Hunter at the Menwith Hill Supporters Club do that I took when the team used to freely mix with the fans, are cherished memories. Rest in Peace TC.

My ambition of getting all the old Leeds songs recorded has taken a step forward after a lot of technical difficulties, hence it has taken so long to get to this stage. The songs are all recorded, and we are now looking at getting them on CDs. As always, things have not been straight forward but keep watching for news of when these will be released.

This new book now completes the series with our first season back in the Premier League, that started in 2016. *The Sleeping Giant Awakens 2016/17; Back to Reality: Leeds United 2017/18; Marcelo Bielsa's Leeds United: Leeds United 2018/19* and *Leeds Are Going to the Premier League! Leeds United Season 2019/20: Promotion in their Centenary Year!* They take you through the journey from a Leeds United fan's perspective travelling to home and away games where hopes were raised before being dashed again. Marcelo Bielsa's arrival at Leeds United started the transformation and brought entertaining football back to Elland Road alongside that fighting spirit and never giving up. It also saw us get promotion back to the Premier League and finally our first season back there although under exceptional circumstances. Before fans could not attend, all home games became a sell out on top of the already sold out away ticket allocations.

All books are available via my publisher JMD Media:
https://www.jmdmedia.co.uk/collections/football-clubs/leeds-united-fc
Meet the author: https://www.jmdmedia.co.uk/pages/heidi-haigh-leeds-united

The new season will start shortly, and it will be a very emotional time with everyone back at games. Look out for that camera and my *Follow Me and Leeds United* blog which will be found on www.followmeandleedsunited.co.uk. Photos from the games will be posted there and I cannot wait to meet up with everyone again.

LUFC – Marching on Together!

ND - #0215 - 270225 - C0 - 234/156/8 - PB - 9781780916262 - Gloss Lamination